THE CLUB ED GUIDE
TO

STARTING AND RUNNING A (PROFITABLE) FREELANCE EDITING BUSINESS

Jennifer Lawler

Please note that the author is not a lawyer or a CPA, nor is she in the business of giving legal or accounting advice. The information provided in this book is general information. The author has tried to be accurate but makes no promises or guarantees. The information in this book assumes a US-based business. Consult with the appropriate experts to be sure you're following your federal and local laws, ordinances, and rules governing business operations.

Table of Contents

Acknowledgments

Many thanks to all of the people who helped bring this book to fruition, including Lynne Baur, who designed the cover, and Linda Formichelli, who provided significant editorial advice.

Other readers and helpers included Ted Hertzog, Jacque Love Hamilton, and Elizabeth Felnagle. Countless editing students and coaching clients have helped me understand the biggest issues facing newer freelancers. Know that I appreciate all of you, named or not!

And special thanks to my daughter Jessica for being my personal cheerleading squad.

Introduction

You Should Be Freelancing (Shouldn't You?)

The other day, I was talking with a friend of mine about the challenges of marketing oneself as a freelancer (consultant, independent contractor, fervent embracer of the gig economy — pick your preference). She mentioned that a business coach once told her the best way to get people to buy your brand when you *are* the brand is to sell your lifestyle as something they, too, can have, if they buy your stuff. Like you can be thin and pretty and wealthy, too, if you go to their ImagineIt! seminar or whatever.

At this point, I started laughing like a hyena.

I think it's fair to say you wouldn't want my life and if you actually lived it for a week, you would show up at my front door demanding to give it back. You might want *parts* of it — like maybe you think it would be great to work from your kitchen table with companionable people you don't actually have to share an office with so you never have to find out how annoying they really are, or maybe you've always wanted to be an editor and help authors bring their visions into reality but have never done so, or possibly you wish the silver in your hair was just as awesome as the silver in mine, and like that.

But there are other parts you wouldn't like, such as the reason I started freelancing in the first place: my daughter was born with a massive brain abnormality and spent large chunks of her early life in hospitals undergoing terrifying surgeries. I didn't become a freelancer because I envisioned myself sipping margaritas by the ocean. I became a freelancer because it was something I could do in a hospital room while waiting for my daughter to wake up from anesthesia.

I know I should share the picture of the ocean-side cabana that I downloaded from iStockphoto.com to convince you that your life would consist of a few hours of effortless work each morning as gentle ocean breezes waft across your smiling face if you would just read my book, but I try not to lie more than I absolutely must. Freelancing is not (necessarily) more fun, glamorous, lucrative, or portable than a staff job.

On the other hand, it is true that a few years ago, I took off for twelve weeks and wandered around Europe and the US with my daughter. A lot of people — more than I can count on both hands and all my toes — wanted to know How I Did It. And the truth is, I couldn't have done it at all if I weren't a freelancer.

For years, I've cordoned off the month of December so that my daughter and I can take memorable holiday trips together. When she was in grade school, I took on fewer projects in the summer months to spend more time with her — while still earning enough to keep us in housing and Disney princess dolls.

Just last year I took four months off work to pursue several creative projects. Freelancing gave me the flexibility (and the cash flow) to make that happen.

As a freelancer, I can turn down projects I'm not interested in doing, I can stop working with people who are a pain in the ass (without having to find a new job), and I'm in charge of how much I earn.

But probably the biggest benefit is this:

A year or two ago, Jessica (my daughter) was seeing her neurosurgeon and the nurse making an appointment for a follow-up visit ushered us out, asking, "Do you need a written excuse for work?"

And for one baffled moment I could not make any sense of what he was saying. I heard the words but they did not compute. I'm a grown adult, so, no, I did not need a freakin' *written excuse* to go about the business of living my life. *What are you even talking about?*

Then I realized that the default mode of operation for corporations is to treat people as if they are incompetent or lying or both. Because that's the only explanation I can figure out for what was clearly a routine question for an exam during business hours. I guess if I were employed in the traditional corporate world, I'd be forced to ask, "Please, boss, can I take my daughter to see the neurosurgeon? Please, can I, please? No? Okay."

Seriously? *Seriously?*

People in the FIRE (Financial Independence, Retire Early) movement are talking primarily about freedom when they talk about the true purpose of FIRE. It's not "retirement" in the sense of not working for an income, but in being able to tell your boss, "Take this job and shove it."

And that's great, but you don't have to be financially independent to do it. You can do it by starting your own side hustle and growing it into a successful business.

And how to do *that* is what this book is all about.

The Context of This Book

This book is for people who are thinking about starting a freelance editing business or who have recently started one and have questions about best practices for going forward.

In this book, I assume that most of your work will be in editing book-length manuscripts. While you could be hired to, say, edit short content pieces for a website, most of the freelance work available for editors is book length. But either way, the basic principles are the same.

I also assume that you plan to (eventually) freelance full-time instead of continuing in your day job, although you may start freelancing as a side hustle. However, the bulk of this book's content applies whether you freelance full or part time.

Most of my experience is in doing (and teaching) developmental editing although I have also done (and taught) copyediting. Lately most of my students and coaching clients have been involved in fiction development, so many of my examples come from that field. But the principles of freelancing I describe in this book apply to any type of editing—developmental editing, copyediting, proofreading — whether for fiction or nonfiction. I will also talk about related areas, such as coaching authors, which you can use to make more money and appeal to a broader range of potential clients.

Finally, I assume you already have or will learn the skills you need to work as an editor. This is not a book on learning the craft. It's about creating a business around the craft. To learn more about the craft of editing (in its many forms), go to the section at the end of this book called "Want More?" or visit the Club Ed website at **www.ClubEdFreelancers.com**.

Some abbreviations I use throughout this book:

AE = acquisitions editor (usually your contact
       person when working for publishers)
CE = copy editor/copyediting
DE = developmental editor/developmental editing,
       sometimes referred to as "dev"
ms = manuscript
mss = manuscripts
WIP = work-in-progress

You'll notice that I talk about two main categories of clients: book publishers and indie authors. In general, most of our clients come from one of these two groups. When I say "book publishers" I mean companies that produce publications. This could be a book packager or a trade magazine publisher or it could even be a commercial press (some provide packaged editorial services to their clients). "Book publishers" is just my shorthand for organizations who hire freelance editors.

"Indie authors" is my name for writers who directly hire you to edit their work, even if they plan to query agents and go the traditional publishing route.

Roles you'll need to understand to be an effective freelance editor include:

- *The acquisitions/assigning editor* is the editor who buys the book or commissions the article/short story. He or she works for a publishing company and may be the one who asks you to do the necessary editing on a project. This person is responsible for shepherding the book through the publishing process, from contracting with the author, to overseeing edits, to approving cover design, to helping coordinate publicity. This role is usually (though not always) played by a staffer. An acquisitions editor is sometimes called a senior editor.

- *Executive editors, editorial directors,* and *editors-in-chief* oversee the big-picture operations of the editorial side of a publishing company and may also be the ones who contract with you to work on a project—but you are most likely to be working with an acquisitions editor.

- *Editors-at-large* are usually brought on by a publisher because they have a specific skill or reputation to contribute. They rarely deal with day-to-day operations and are usually not on staff. As a freelance editor, you will rarely work with an editor-at-large—but you may *be* an editor-at-large.

- *Managing editors* are more likely to be found in periodical publishing than in book publishing, and may perform many of the same roles as the acquisitions editor. In some cases, the managing editor functions more like a copy editor. In book publishing, managing editors tend to play a role similar to executive editor and may have editors reporting to them. Sometimes they will be more like a production editor. In any case, they will almost always be on staff.

- *A production editor* oversees the physical production of a book or magazine. This editor usually works closely with the managing editor or acquisitions editor to produce the publication or book. Most production editing positions are staff positions, and they require a specific expertise in project management.

- *The developmental editor*, also called content editor or substantive editor, is one who works at the big-picture level. Does the ms do what it's supposed to do? The developmental editor may also perform basic fact-checking and will be expected to catch discrepancies such as the protagonist who has blue eyes in the first chapter but brown eyes in the second. Developmental editing is often done by an assigning or acquisitions editor, but it can be farmed out to freelancers.

- *A copy editor* is also concerned with whether a piece works, but this is at the sentence level—polishing the prose. The copy editor also ensures the ms conforms to the accepted style.

- *The proofreader*, which many people confuse with the copy editor, is the final defense against error in a manuscript. The proofreader goes through a manuscript before it is published to make sure that no errors have slipped through after editing. A proofreader may compare a final typeset work against its copyedited draft to make sure the changes were accurately reflected in the final. This work requires an excellent eye for detail.

Developmental editing, copyediting, and proof-reading are the three areas with the most potential for freelancers.

Gut-Check Checklist

If you've had a staff editing job, taken an editing class or two, or edited a friend's newsletter — in other words, you possess at least a basic grasp of the craft — you might be thinking about turning your skills into a side hustle or even a full-time freelancing business.

Before you quit your day job, make sure you understand what you're getting into. You have to ask yourself, in a no-bullshit way, if you're cut out for freelancing — and if you're not, are you okay with sticking to staff jobs, or do you want to work on your skills so you can become a successful full-time freelancer?

Some people find the be-your-own-boss part hard. They need the structure of a staff job and the accountability of reporting to a boss. Others don't like the isolation of freelancing. No shame in that. Freelancing is not for everyone.

Below are some questions to ask yourself before giddy dreams of ocean-front cabanas short-circuit your common sense.

Why Are You Freelancing?

Before committing time, money, and effort to starting your editing business, ask yourself why you want to. This is where you need to apply brutal honesty to your motives. Is it because you're tired of working hard? Most self-employed business owners work longer hours than their corporate counterparts (and, sorry to say, actually earn less). If you're tired of working fifty hours a week, consider that on average full-time freelancers work sixty hours a week.

However, the upside is the flexibility. You can work in your pajamas. You can cook breakfast for your kids every morning. You can work at midnight if that's how your schedule shakes out. If you want to take a day off and go to the zoo, you can. (You just don't get to take a paid vacation day to do it.)

Most people choose to become self-employed because they reach a point where they can no longer stand fitting into a corporate world that doesn't suit them. They want to be their own boss. They want to pick what work they'll do and turn down projects that don't appeal to them. They want more control over their work lives and more say in how their work and personal lives intersect. They understand the amount of work involved and have prepared for it.

Do You Have Experience?

In my consulting work — I advise freelance editors on how to be more successful in their businesses — I often encounter aspiring editors who spend years taking classes before they feel ready to tackle an actual project. Some of them never feel ready. Before you plunge into freelance editing, you do have to gain knowledge of your field. But you also need *experience*, which you can't get just by taking classes. You have to go out and do some editing—either through a staff job or internship or on the side until you're experienced enough to charge professional rates.

Editing is not an entry-level position. You have to have knowledge and experience to succeed at it as a freelancer. I'll talk about how to get more experience throughout this book, but if you have literally none, you're not ready to strike out on your own just yet.

Are You a Self-Starter?

I talked about freedom and flexibility being key reasons why I'm a freelancer and have been for more than twenty years. But if you're too focused on that aspect, you'll piss away days, weeks, and months without actually building a business. Are you (or can you be) a self-starter? Can you motivate yourself to get out of bed day after day even if there are no immediate consequences if you don't?

It may sound like paradise to be free of your inconsiderate boss and unkind co-workers, but they'll be replaced by inconsiderate and unkind clients— freelancing is not some miracle cure for everything that's wrong with your life. Are you able to work hard every day even if you're the only one who sees you crushing it?

Do You Need a Steady Paycheck?

Which leads to the next point to consider. How much do you need the security of a predictable income? If you're already living on the edge, paycheck-to-paycheck, you can't just chuck the job and expect freelancing to take up the slack right away. It can take time—months—before you establish any kind of reliable income from your efforts. If you don't mind feast one week and famine the next, or you've socked away savings, or you hooked up with a life partner willing to take on more of the financial burden while you're getting established, you'll find it easier to start your own editing business.

Consider your financial goals for the next few years. Are you planning to buy a house? Self-employed people can have trouble getting home loans unless they've been in business for at least five years and show tax returns indicating consistent income. If you're planning on making major purchases in the next few years, either reconsider the purchases themselves or think about staying with your present position until after you've secured the loan or made the purchase.

Do You Need Benefits?

Related to the "steady paycheck" concept is the "perks" concept. Will you need the benefits that come with a staff job, such as health insurance or retirement benefits? With healthcare in the US in a transition period, it can be hard to know whether you'll be able to get health insurance on the open market in the coming years. If you're near retirement or close to being vested in a retirement program, you might be wise to wait a few years because of the financial benefits that would be yours if you stayed.

Does Your Family Support This?

Freelancers like going it alone, but if you have a spouse and/or children, you'll need them on board, too. Though your ultimate goal may be to have more flexibility in your life, in the beginning you may actually have less, especially if you're starting with a side hustle in addition to your regular job.

Some people gain the support of their families by negotiating a deadline: They'll start contributing steady income to the household by a specific date. If they can't meet the deadline, they return to their former career. (This works best if you can return to your former career. In other words, don't burn your bridges.) The downside to this approach is that freelancing requires time and persistence to work (sometimes a lot of time and persistence). Make sure you give yourself every opportunity to succeed.

Although you need to have a plan in place in case you fail, you must also be convinced that you won't, and that any failure you have right now is just temporary. Mindset is everything, so if you're surrounded by naysayers, it will be a tougher slog than it needs to be. Do what you can to gain the support of your significant others.

Is Your Personality Suited to It?

If you're a security-oriented person who hates taking risks, keeping your day job and working a side hustle may be the best solution (unless you're trying to break your addiction to security). One talented colleague found she didn't have the stomach for the tension that surrounded her when she tried freelancing — getting clients, dealing with last-minute cancellations and payment problems, erratic workflow. Her spouse wasn't exactly helpful, either. She still enjoys giving critiques to writer friends but no longer tries to make a business out of it.

Think about how you'll deal with working alone. Can you do it day after day, week after week, month after month without starting to talk to the wallpaper? You must not only tolerate working alone, you must enjoy it. If you don't love working alone, you'll be seeking excuses to get away from working. Then you'll be going to lunch with your mother or shopping with friends instead of finishing the project that's due tomorrow.

Support from friends and colleagues can help you weather the isolation but if the very thought of eating lunch by yourself every day makes you sad, you may want to rethink freelancing.

Chapter 1

Getting Started

Now I'm going to go a little New Age on you and talk about the touchy-feely parts of freelancing. It's more important to your success to know your *why* than it is to choose the best invoicing platform for your needs, so I'm going to start there. We'll get to the exciting topics of business licenses and estimated tax payments a little later (Chapters 6 and 7, also known as The Paperwork Parts).

Purpose Equals Prospects

Here's one of my favorite phrases to use with newer freelancers: "Purpose Equals Prospects." I sound like a multilevel marketer, don't I? Please forgive me. But this is not a con job: before you spend much time starting and building your editing business, you have to figure out what your business is for. I don't mean, "I'm a freelance developmental editor." Or "my business is copyediting for a variety of publishers." I mean, what is your *purpose*?

Mine is to help women find a way to tell their stories. That gets me out of bed a lot faster than, "Oh, great, six more manuscripts to edit this month" does. Now, I don't necessarily share this purpose on every Facebook post I make. I use it to shape my actions, not as a marketing slogan.

Purpose Guides Decision-Making

This doesn't mean that I won't help men or that I won't edit a how-to guide that has nothing to do with anyone telling any story. It just means that this purpose informs my decision-making regarding my work. It guides my marketing and my messaging to potential clients.

In my purpose you'll see my target audience: women who have stories to tell and for one reason or another are having trouble telling them (implied by the "find a way"). It doesn't limit me to a specific approach: I do as much coaching, hand-holding, and cheerleading as I do actual developmental editing.

I help people figure out who their audience is, I help them figure out how to reach that audience, I help them conceptualize their books—I do all kinds of things that don't necessarily equal "developmental editing," even though I say I'm a developmental editor.

I have a colleague whose purpose is, "To help people share their expertise in the most effective way to accomplish their goals and reach their audience."

You can tell right off that we appeal to different types of clients.

So the first thing I want you to do is figure out what your purpose is. Don't worry; this can change as you do. I used to be more pragmatic and less touchy-feely.

Back then my purpose was more like, "Organize the hell out of these people and get their work to production."

What would you like your freelance work to be, not just for your clients but for you? Your purpose can be to attract lucrative projects that challenge your skills, or to provide a service to emerging authors who are struggling to find their voices, or to champion the work of people of color, or whatever makes Monday morning worth showering for. It can be anything. But it needs to be something.

Finding Your Purpose

I'm not going to give you a ton of guidance regarding how to state your purpose. That's up to you. I don't care how many active verbs your purpose contains or anything like that. I just want you to have one. It doesn't have to be especially brilliant or even terribly unique. What you start out with may not be what you end up with by the time you've finished reading this book. That's fine. But having at least a general sense of purpose helps you figure out who your potential clients will be, which is a critical step in building your business.

Don't get too caught up in the mystique of the word "purpose." It's not as if the universe knows it and you don't until you pass some kind of spiritual test. No quests are required. A purpose can be, and often is, simply something you decide based on things you've enjoyed doing in the past or have had success with:

"You know, I really liked working with Aunt Emma on her memoir." Bingo.

Think about the type of audience/client you're trying to reach — "women" for me; "experts in their field" for my colleague. And you should give some attention to the type of problem you're solving ("teaching them how to communicate the importance of their research to the general public" or "crafting emotionally resonant fiction").

Other than that, it can be anything that you find compelling enough to get out of bed to do.

What Do You Want From Your Work?

Maybe you don't know what your purpose is. Maybe you don't care. Maybe you don't connect with one purpose over another — helping newly minted memoirists get their words on the page is no more or less compelling to you than helping bestselling novelists polish their prose. Maybe the whole thought of identifying a purpose makes you roll your eyes.

In that case, forget about purpose. Think about what you want from your business. This is another way of figuring out who your potential clients might be and how you might reach them.

Suppose you want to make a comfortable amount of money while maintaining a flexible schedule and that's really all you care about. If you can collect six figures a year (or whatever "comfortable" means to you) then you're all set. The business is just a means to an end.

That's certainly fine and perfectly acceptable. But it means you need to find clients who will pay top dollar for your work. It means you need to focus on developing ongoing relationships with clients who can hire you for repeat business (less time spent marketing) and who have bigger budgets, so this is likely to be corporations or else a very select group of individuals with lots of discretionary income and a recurring need for editing.

Or perhaps you want your freelance editing to feel personally satisfying, for you to feel you're making a difference in people's lives. If so, you're probably going to want to work directly with indie authors rather than freelancing for publishers.

Even if you do know what your purpose is, knowing what you want from your business helps you figure out the types of clients you need to target (and how to find them).

Identifying Your Potential Clients

Think about what your purpose implies (if not outright states) about your audience (potential clients). My audience (in very general terms) is women telling stories. When I reflect on this, I realize I care about the kinds of stories they're trying to tell. I want to help them tell stories about their own lives, or from their own imaginations, so that suggests memoir and fiction.

I'm not interested in helping a woman tell someone else's story (biography or history), no matter how noble a cause that may be. I do edit a fair amount of nonfiction but that is an artifact of an earlier purpose; I'm good at it but don't actively pursue those types of clients.

So I'm looking for women who are writing memoirs and fiction. As I said above, my purpose also implies they're having trouble telling those stories. Some further reflection on this tells me that I don't want to work with writers who are blocked, or who are struggling with serious mental or emotional problems that are getting in their way. I'm simply not equipped to deal with these issues. Rather, I want to work with writers who are doubting themselves or don't yet have the skillset to successfully convey their vision. I have the ability and knowledge to help these people. One main way I do this is by helping writers figure out what the story is and to dig deep to get it out. In other words, I help them learn craft.

Additionally, I'm not interested in working with people who treat writing as a hobby. I want to work with serious students of writing. Therefore my audience is professional women committed to learning craft to tell their stories.

You might reach entirely different conclusions and that's fine and wonderful! I'm just explaining how this process worked for me.

I recognized that there were a number of women I knew who, like me, had had success as nonfiction writers, but wanted to spend more time working on their fiction. However, the skills of nonfiction and fiction are different, and professional writers can struggle with the transition. So I became a guide for helping women shift from writing nonfiction to writing fiction or creative nonfiction.

Narrow = Clear

Now, this may seem like a very narrow group, but that's a good thing! Later I'll talk more about the importance of specialization and finding your niche(s). But for now just realize that having a narrow potential audience/clientele is not a problem but an asset. The more you can pinpoint exactly who your ideal client is, the easier it is to find her and let her know what your fees are for helping her solve her problem.

I know exactly where to find the people I've defined as my ideal client type. I'm already Facebook friends with them. I'm in the same writers' groups as they are. I go to the same conferences. Mostly I simply let people know that this is the work I do and they come find me (more on networking and referrals in a bit).

Now, let's see about applying this process to someone who isn't me.

Suppose your purpose is to help emerging writers find their voices. You think about this for a while and you decide that you love working with teens, and so you would like to start coaching teen writers at the library. You know exactly where to find the library and also you have a good sense of where you might find teen writers—at the local high school. So, you could reach out to them and tell them about your services.

One Question You Must Ask

But before you do that, the question you must ask yourself is, "Can this clientele pay a fair market value for my services?" Because if the answer is no, you don't have a business, you have a hobby. Or, possibly a nonprofit organization funded by arts grants but that is outside my realm of expertise so let's just assume you're as profit-motivated as I am.

Teens writing novels don't have any money to spend on your services. Their parents might but it is doubtful that they would dig very deep or very often. So while this could be a nice gig you do on the side because you love to see thirteen-year-olds realize they have potential, you'll have to revisit your purpose insofar as profit motive is concerned.

What kinds of emerging writers could afford your services? Who else might want to learn to tell stories? What about retirees interested in the legacy they are leaving? "Legacy" isn't just about their estate. Maybe they want to share what they know or give their children a better sense of what their lives were like. Retirees are much more likely to have disposable income and be willing to spend it on something as important to them as a story they want to leave behind. Can you think of where you might find these potential clients? The senior center, the Osher Institute, next door?

Niches and Specialization

Often beginning freelancers will come to me saying they're not sure how to get clients. They're willing to do just about anything for just about any price to get things rolling, so where can they find someone who needs an editor?

The answer is everywhere and nowhere, or, more specifically, I have no idea.

Back when I used to do more writing than editing, I had a specific niche. I was the queen of martial arts writing. I never wanted to be the queen of martial arts writing, but that is how my career evolved because:

1. I had an interest in martial arts.
2. I had a unique (at the time) perspective on martial arts.
3. I was able to string sentences together without hurting myself.

All of that meant that people would pay me a lot of money to write about martial arts and almost none to write about other things. That's when I began to see that, Heinlein notwithstanding, specialization is as important for people as it is for insects.

Instead of writing anything about anything, I wrote about women and martial arts. I used many different angles, but basically it came down to women and martial arts. So my audience was women in martial arts. I knew where to find this audience. I was involved in martial arts. I took the same classes they did, read the same magazines they read, watched the same videos they watched, encountered the same attitudes they encountered. I was one of them. I got asked to speak, to guest-teach, to write. Everything reinforced everything else.

Instead of struggling against the fact that people with cash in hand wanted me to write about martial arts, I embraced the idea. Instead of trying to write anything about anything for anyone, I focused on my niche.

I do the same now as an editor. Instead of trying to edit anything for anyone, I target second-act women writers who are professionals transitioning from writing nonfiction to writing fiction. That seems highly specialized, and it is. That's not to say all of my clients fall into this category. Many do; many don't. It just gives me something to wrap my mind around when it comes time to spread the word about what I do. (I also work with a lot of publishing and packaging companies, and I'll explain more about how to do that later.)

Finding Your Niche

Sometimes you know exactly the kind of work you want to be doing. Maybe it's something you love: You love mysteries and you want to help mystery writers write the best books possible. Or maybe it's something you have suitable credentials to do: You have a degree in biology and you want to work with science writers or science textbook publishers.

If you've identified your purpose ("helping retirees write the stories of their lives") your niche will sometimes be fairly obvious—it's written in your purpose. But when it's not as obvious, you have to figure out what your niche is.

Remember my friend whose purpose is "To help people share their expertise in the most effective way to accomplish their goals and reach their audience"? Her audience, as stated, is "people." That's not enough of a niche. But "expertise" is also a qualification mentioned. So, her niche is working with experts. What kinds of experts? She would have to look at her credentials, past experience, and interests to narrow this down.

Narrowing Your Niche

Knowing your area of specialization helps you get closer to identifying your potential audience/clientele, but your niche may not be narrow enough to truly help you find your people. Consider this: my stated story preferences—memoir and fiction—encompass a fairly enormous range. I can't possibly know everything about it all. (This is one reason why specialization is so important).

So if I look a little closer at my own background, it's obvious that most of my experience is in editing romance. I enjoy thrillers just as much as the next person, but it's romance that I know and it's romance that everyone knows about me, so guess what genre I talk about editing?

The advantage of this approach is that if you're consistent, then everyone eventually knows you as the person who does X. I'm the person who helps second-act professional nonfiction writers (who are women) learn to write romance.

What's your thing? Ideally it's connected with something you already do. It can be something very simple. For example, if you already read mysteries, you're more likely to be a good mystery editor than someone who doesn't read mysteries (plus, you'll probably enjoy the work).

What direction do the skills you currently have push you in? If you already copyedit memoirs for a publishing company then it isn't a huge stretch to think you could start developmental editing them.

Identifying What Makes Your Work Valuable

Once you know the niche you're going to target, you need to show potential clients that you have something valuable to offer them. Potential clients don't care that you love to edit and want to start a successful editing business. Potential clients only care about how you can help them. That is, a potential client has a problem. You need to be the solution (that is, "you have something valuable to offer them").

The corollary is that if potential clients don't think they have a problem, then you're not a solution. Some people try to convince potential clients that they *do* have a problem ("Readers hate to read books riddled with errors!") but I find this too quixotic for my tastes—why spend time trying to convince people that they need my services when I could spend that time connecting with people who already know they need my services?

In other words, I prefer engaging with potential clients who already know they have a problem (a manuscript in need of an editor). Then all I have to do is show them how I'm the solution.

Your Personal Inventory

Think about what you already know—what your skillset is and how those skills might help a potential client. Conduct a personal inventory. What skills and experiences do you currently have that you can capitalize on as a freelance editor?

For example, if you spent a couple years as a newspaper reporter covering the city council, then you almost certainly know how to explain complex issues to nonspecialists. Perhaps you can edit the local university's press releases to help spread the word about their research.

Look at your education. This is not the most important selling point for any client, but a degree in English, journalism, or linguistics indicates an interest in language that could translate to editing. Classes and workshops in various editing-related skills can serve as credentials.

Next, consider how you've used your skills to help others. Have you critiqued fiction for friends? Edited the newsletter for a volunteer job? Taught grammar and usage to kids in your sixth-grade class? Think about any potentially relevant special skills and experiences. Have you written and published fiction? Then you understand the process.

Record Your Experience—All of It

Whenever you gain any kind of relevant experience or education, note it on an accomplishments list. Record even minor projects you've done, awards you've won (no matter how local or trivial they seem to be), anything that adds to your credentials. You won't share these accomplishments with everyone — "I won my writing group's award for best new erotica!"

probably doesn't need to be shared with your corporate clients.

But you'd be surprised at how quickly you can forget things you've done. Your accomplishment list can come in handy later when a potential client says, "We're looking for someone who has worked on short stories." A quick glance at your list can remind you that five years ago you edited an anthology.

When you gain experience in your field, keep the relevant supporting information readily available. If you start editing the company newsletter, save copies of/links to each issue to show to prospective clients. Screenshots can prove a book you edited was a #1 Amazon bestseller for a brief, glorious moment in time.

Ask for letters of recommendation or testimonials when appropriate. Get permission to give names of current clients to prospective clients.

Update Your Resume/Bio Sheet

Separate from your accomplishment list, keep a resume and/or a bio sheet specific to your niche.

A *resume* lists education and employment history in a format designed to highlight dates, job titles, and responsibilities.

A *bio sheet* consists of several descriptive paragraphs about who you are and what you do. The bio sheet can reflect more of your personality, interests, and aspirations, whereas a resume primarily communicates career facts.

Depending on your potential clientele, one might be more useful than another or both may be necessary.

Every few months, go through your accomplishments list and update your resume/bio sheet as appropriate.

Most freelancers have several resumes/bio sheets, each of which highlights different aspects of their experience. When I'm showing my nonfiction editing experience, I use one resume. When I'm showing my fiction editing experience, I use a different one.

Having an organized, easy-to-understand way to present your experience and your projects helps turn potential clients into actual clients.

Gaining Experience

You may feel that "I know each and every critical failing of *Star Trek: the Next Generation*" isn't likely to solve anyone's problems and you may be right. But it's a start.

Consider getting some real-life experience under your belt if you have very little right now. When I first started out, I bartered editing and writing services for things I wanted, like a membership at a local gym.

Always think in terms of exchange. Even if you're not the most experienced editor in the world, your time is worth something. Editing for free just because you want the experience devalues your work.

Instead, offer your services in exchange for something else, not necessarily money. For example, you might edit a manuscript for a friend in exchange for her babysitting your kids a certain number of hours. You're both giving and getting something of value, even if no cash changes hands. You may do a few initial projects for low pay and a testimonial.

Think Through All the Options

Some experts discourage people from working for friends and family. They have a valid point. You end up doing work for free or for less than market value when you should be doing work for pay. You're frustrated and your father-in-law is unhappy with what you've done. However, in the beginning, when you have no business and precious little experience, you must start somewhere, so don't rule anything out without giving it some careful thought first.

If you haven't quit your day job, make a point of getting relevant experience before you head out on your own. Are there any opportunities where you work to pick up editing credentials? Even something as simple as editing the company newsletter counts. Although it may not seem possible at first glance, your current employer may be your best bet for gaining relevant experience before you start working full-time at your business.

A Few Friendly Warnings

If you're just starting out and have little relevant experience, don't invent some, thinking no one will ever find out and if they do, they'll overlook it because you're so talented. Freelancers build relationships based on trust and no matter how talented you are, if you betray that trust, your clients will drop you. They may even go to great lengths to spread the word about your misrepresentations. The last thing you need is for someone to crank up the Twitter outrage machine and feed it your name.

By the same token, sometimes freelancers are so eager to take on any project that they agree to do things outside their ability. Stretching yourself is fine. Learning new things is terrific — we should all do more of it.

Promising something you have no way to adequately deliver is not okay.

If you have experience copyediting user manuals, it's not much of a stretch to also copyedit how-to books. But it's another thing entirely to agree to, say, coach a novelist on figuring out the narrative arc of her work-in-progress. In other words, A to B makes sense. A to E does not.

Use what experience you do have to make logical bridges to related areas. You can find ways to connect where you are (A) to where you want to be (E) but it requires time and planning, not shortcuts. So far in life there is no such thing as a teleporter.

Chapter 2

To Market, To Market

Freelance editors who build successful businesses seek long-term client relationships that involve repeat business. A private-pay individual (such as an indie author) who hires you to edit four novels a year at $2000 per edit will be a bigger boost to your bottom line than the one who hires you to edit a $3000 project once.

How you find these long-term clients is through marketing and promotion — not to mention doing good work once you've been hired!

Marketing is, generally, all the actions related to creating a demand for your services, which might include anything from researching customer needs to buying advertisements. Promotion and publicity — building awareness of your services — are subsets of marketing.

Many freelancers rely on low- or no-cost promotion to get clients but if they're not aware of larger principles (like knowing what potential clients want/need) their efforts are less likely to succeed.

Designing Your Marketing Roadmap

Like anyone else, your overall business goal is to generate revenue, but "I'd like some money, please," is a desire, not a roadmap.

In other words, you have to figure out what steps you can take in order to make the money, which means designing your marketing roadmap. That requires breaking your goal/desire down into parts:

- strategies (guiding principles)
- tactics (ways to implement the guiding principles)
- actions (to-do list items)

To make money, you need to get people to hire you. So how do you do that?

You could probably come up with a hundred and eleven possibilities if you put your mind to it (post flyers at the local coffee shop, hire a skywriter) but unless you want to spend your life bouncing around from coffee shop to airfield, you need a strategy — that is, you need a guiding principle for how you do your marketing.

For example, my overall strategy for getting editing projects (whether from indie authors or publishing companies) is to hang out with people in publishing. Literally my job is to make friends. Whenever I look at how I get clients, there's almost always a name involved: Michele or Linda or Jerri. Someone I know referred the client to me.

I've spent much of my work life participating in writers' conferences, belonging to writers' and editors' organizations, and connecting people to other people. (And, in case you were wondering, I'm a card-carrying member of Introverts United!)

So let's break this down. The strategy is "hang out with people in publishing." The tactics are going to conferences and joining organizations. The action/to-do items are "send in my membership application" and "book my flight to New York."

That means when I'm planning my marketing, "hang out with people in publishing" is always on my mind. Because most of my clients are publishing companies, I don't have to "find out my clients' needs"—they know they need developmental editors, and, hey, I'm a developmental editor. But it's not always that simple.

Suppose you want to work with indie authors. To reach them, an overall strategy might be "use social media to get clients." Tactics might be to interact with potential clients on Twitter and Facebook. Specific to-do items might be "retweet or respond to potential clients' tweets ten times per day" and "research whether a Facebook group or page would be a better way to showcase my business."

But when developing tactics, you need to think very carefully about how you interact with your potential clients. If you say, "Hi, I'm a book development editor!" that may not communicate anything to them. But if you say, "I help indie authors tell their stories in an emotionally engaging way," that might make a potential client pause and say, "Hmm."

It's even better if you can break it down further: "I show book authors how to hook the reader from the first page" tells me something that "I work with authors to improve their pacing" simply doesn't.

Picking Successful Strategies

How do you decide what types of marketing strategies are likely to succeed? You have to know something about your potential clients.

In Chapter 1, I talked about how your purpose equals your prospects. If your purpose is to help seniors tell their stories, you're probably not going to find them on Instagram, so using social media may not be your best strategy.

Instead, you might focus on making connections with seniors in your local community (this would be your strategy). A tactic might be to work with program directors at various senior services, such as a local senior outreach center or continuing education programs for seniors like Osher. To-do list items might include attending a senior center open house to meet staff or developing a class proposal to present at Osher.

Tailoring your strategies to where you'll find your audience is just one aspect of developing appropriate marketing strategies. Another aspect is to consider your own preferences and inclinations. Hate social media? Then "use social media to get clients" is probably not a good strategy for you. That's fine! Ruling things out helps you focus on what is more likely to work for you.

Once you've identified overall marketing strategies, your tactics and action items naturally flow from there.

Assessing Your Strategies

As you're working out what your marketing strategy/strategies will be, make sure you're assessing them for viability before you get too far along. "Making connections with local seniors" may be a fruitful strategy with virtually limitless possibilities in New York City, but in Eudora, Kansas, there are many fewer potential clients. Once this pool is exhausted, what are you going to do?

That doesn't mean you should abandon your plan— maybe the first stage of your effort can be to work locally before you expand regionally. But the more you can anticipate potential problems ahead of time, the better you can plan to adapt to them.

One way to do this is to research based on your proposed strategy. "Make connections with local seniors" seems to beg for you to find out how many seniors live in the area.

The most recent census tells us just over six thousand people live in Eudora. Of these, fewer than ten percent are age sixty-five and older ("seniors"). So, about six hundred people might be potential clients. But out of six hundred people, how many of them actually need an editor? Even if we optimistically say that ten percent will need an editor, ten percent is only sixty people!

Try this on for size: Visualize your high school graduating class. Of those three hundred or one thousand people, how many do you suppose have gone on to write books and hire editors for them? Right, not that many.

Because we're editors and we're surrounded by people who love words, we forget that in the wider world, what we do is somewhat specialized to begin with. So, be realistic about strategies that target a general population ("local seniors"). Recognize that you may need to use intermediate steps between "let local seniors know I exist" and "edit memoirs for local seniors."

These intermediate steps might include planning and presenting programs that introduce seniors to the idea of writing a memoir—for example, a class with the message, "Your family wants to hear your story." You might even make this less intimidating by teaching something easy to wrap one's mind around, like "Five-Minute Memoir."

Post-Launch Assessment

After you've worked your chosen marketing strategy for a while (say, three to six months), you need to assess whether it's working for you. Is the overall strategy effective? You'll know the answer by looking at your income. If you're not acquiring clients and billing them after three to six months of trying, you have a problem.

Let me add: Success doesn't happen overnight. I'm not saying you should be booked wall to wall within ten minutes of hanging out your shingle. I am saying that if you've been in business three to six months and you're still waiting for your first client, something's wrong.

When you're starting out, "I sent ten letters of introduction to publishing companies" is the only proxy for success you have. But at some point those LOIs should be landing clients. If not, there's something wrong with your letter, your offer, or your credentials.

In my work with freelancers, I've found two common reasons for lack of success are (1) the freelancer isn't trying hard enough and (2) the freelancer is trying hard at the wrong things.

You know how to fix (1). You can't expect to succeed in a competitive industry like freelance editing if you're devoting an hour a week to the process. For (2), the solution is to reassess what you're doing and try something else.

Sometimes the answer to the question, "Is this thing working?" is neither, "Yes, my marketing strategy works great!" or "No, my marketing strategy doesn't work at all," the answer is, "My strategy has so-so effectiveness." If that's the case for you, welcome to the club. This is true of most strategies and it's an extremely frustrating position to be in. If the answer is yes/no, the solution is obvious. If the answer is "sort of," the solution is not obvious.

Ask yourself, Are there ways to increase the flow of work through this channel/strategy? What are these ways? If not, are there other strategies you should try?

In the case of the Eudora seniors, one might widen the strategy to include the region. With Kansas City and Lawrence within twenty minutes' drive, suddenly the pool of potential local seniors becomes a lot larger. About 2.5 million people live in this area, and about twelve percent (300,000) are seniors, making this a much bigger potential opportunity.

Finding Your Mentors

Every successful freelancer I've ever met has had a mentor or at least a group of more experienced colleagues who helped. They may not have had the editorial equivalent of Obi-Wan teaching them how to use the light saber, but they had access to people who showed them the ropes, even if the rope-showers didn't do it in person (a colleague/mentor on Facebook) and even if the rope-showers didn't know they were doing it (an expert who wrote a book).

As you work on building your business, you'll ask fellow freelancers for advice, read their blogs and books, join their groups. But be certain that the people whose advice you take understand the business. One consultant I know of advised a newer editor to approach people at a conference and ask them the names of the clients they worked with. The new editor felt hurt and frustrated when people ignored her question or gave her the brush-off.

An experienced consultant would have known that most established editors don't share client names with people they don't know, except in the generic sense of "I've done work for Simon & Schuster."

First reason why not: the implied consent to act as a reference, which most professionals will not do for someone whose work they do not know.

Second: the professional worked hard to establish that relationship and to maintain it. She's not going to give access away to the competition without a darned good reason.

Third: confidentiality. Most people don't want their editors blathering on about their projects to strangers.

In some cases, editors are asked to keep their involvement quiet.

Finally: lack of reciprocation. Established colleagues may trade client information if doing so will be mutually beneficial. Networking is not about taking everything you can get from other people but about establishing relationships with people. The only reason a newer editor would ask an established professional for a client name is in order to pitch that client. What does the established professional get in exchange for this? Nothing.

Instead, the newer editor should have been advised to ask how the established professionals got their first client (or their biggest client or whatever is of interest). This is an easier ask for the professional to deliver on and most will be happy to talk freely about the hows.

The difference between the two pieces of advice ("ask the name of their clients," and "ask how they got their clients") is extremely important. And that's what you consult advisors and consultants for—to know the nuances, the ins and outs, the customs and culture of the profession you need advice about.

So, choose your mentors wisely. How much experience do they have? Do they have experience that directly relates to what you're trying to do? Do they assume that their personal experience is directly applicable to everyone else or do they have a sense of context? In other words, a "mentor" who thinks all editors should edit in exactly the same way doesn't understand editing.

Competition or Colleagues?

Your business doesn't exist in a vacuum, so you have to think about your competition. Let's face it, lots of people want to make a living working from home in their bunny slippers. Many of these people call themselves freelance editors. Further, many of them have clients who don't have any idea how to assess the quality of their work—how many beginning writers can judge good editing? The number is probably even smaller than you think.

So, being great at what you do is no guarantee of success. Complicating matters further, many freelancers don't need to make a living wage—they're just doing this as a hobby or to bring in some extra cash without having to go out to a second job. Someone freelancing as a side hustle can charge low fees and not wonder how she's going to keep a roof over her head.

It can feel dispiriting to see literally thousands of freelancers advertising their services online, wondering how you can possibly get anyone to pay attention to you, particularly if you plan to charge enough to keep yourself adequately supplied with chocolate and tea.

But I have some good news. People undercharging for their work are not your competition. (At least, they shouldn't be!) And the people who don't know what quality work is are not your market. (At least, they shouldn't be!) Ergo (I love that word), the freelancers catering to them are not your competition, either.

With that slight adjustment, I've slashed your competition by ninety percent. But that remaining ten percent—they're the *real* competition. They're experienced professionals who've been at this a long time and they are smart, wily, and protective of their clients.

They're also your colleagues! Your soon-to-be friends! They're the people who can teach you how to thrive. That's because they know this is not a zero-sum game. They don't believe that if you get something that means they lose something (at least, most of them don't think this way). They believe there's enough to go around. And they're right. If you're a dedicated, talented professional, there's plenty of work for you.

Look at it this way. Twenty years ago, when I got into this business, I worked for certain kinds of clients because I was a match for those clients. They didn't have enormous budgets and I didn't have a ton of experience. But at some point we stopped being a match. Their budgets didn't get any bigger but I got more experience, so I could go on to other clients who did have bigger budgets. My doing so left a gap: those former clients of mine still needed someone to edit for them.

Enter the less-experienced editor who is just starting out.

When I left those clients, I was leaving on good terms — I didn't hate them, I just was moving on to new and better-paying challenges. When possible, I would give them names of people I knew would be glad to have the work.

I was also the recipient of this type of largesse. When my more-experienced colleagues went on to greener pastures, they'd often recommend me for the work they were leaving behind. That's how it works, or can work, if you think of other editors as your colleagues, not your competition.

Beyond establishing friendly relations with your competition/colleagues, focus on honing those aspects of your editorial talents that will distinguish you from other editors.

Earlier, I talked a bit about specialization. It's a good way for you to define your market so you know where to find potential clients.

It's also a way to help you stand out from the crowd—from the competition. If I'm looking for someone to edit my dystopian new adult science fiction novel, an editor chirping "I can edit anything for anyone!" doesn't even register on my awareness. I'm looking for someone with more specialized expertise than that. Don't be afraid that you'll miss opportunities if you specialize; be worried that you'll miss opportunities if you don't.

Who You Get to Know

I've always said that success isn't about who you know, it's about who you get to know. I grew up in suburban Kansas (yes, there is such a thing as suburban Kansas). Now I live in small-city Kansas (yes, there are cities in Kansas). It wasn't like anyone I knew when I was growing up and starting out had the slightest idea what a book editor did. But while I didn't know anyone who could hook me up with editing clients, I did know a lot of people who knew about building businesses, and I "knew" people who wrote books on writing and publishing, and I had a couple of teachers who thought I could do anything, and that was where I started, and it was more than enough.

Certainly it would have been easier if I'd grown up in Manhattan with a father who was a publishing lawyer and a mother who was a literary agent, but most of us don't, so we have to figure out other ways to succeed.

Start with where you are. Think of the people you know, even the ones loosely affiliated with you, like Facebook friends or LinkedIn connections. Consider ways you can get help from these people. I don't mean sending them urgent messages asking them to hire you or refer clients to you. I mean asking them to give you feedback on your rates or to remind you of the title of the business book they were raving about last week. I mean getting them involved and invested in your success (which means you need to be involved and invested in theirs, too!)

How to Ask

Know the limits of collegiality. "How do I start a freelance editing business?" is the kind of email message that makes me roll my eyes. (Although from now on, I'll roll my eyes and then send a link to where they can purchase this book.)

"I'm starting a freelance editing business and was wondering if you could take a peek at my website and let me know whether the description of services is clear" is something I would do, especially if I knew the person (no matter how barely) who was asking.

People like to make things happen but you have to help them help you. I have received emails from random people I don't know stating, "I'm starting a freelance editing business. Please send me any authors you can't help." The chances of this happening are zero.

I've also gotten emails like this: "I've been following your SOCIAL MEDIA feed and I've found your tips for developmental editors to be extremely helpful. I know you must get a lot of inquiries from authors who don't end up being a good match for you. I'm starting a freelance editing business and I'd be honored if you'd consider referring those types of inquiries to me. I have taken NAME OF editing classes from NAME OF REPUTABLE INSTITUTION OR INSTRUCTOR and have gotten excellent reviews from my current clients. One calls me 'the kind of editor who knows what you're trying to say even when you don't.' I edit GENRES and my website is www.SmartEditor.com. I'd be happy to answer any questions you might have about my experience and expertise."

That is a lot more likely to get attention from me. It shows that the editor has spent some time thinking about what I would need to know to make a referral.

I have a list of people I refer projects to. This is one way to get on it. If nothing else, an email like this would prompt me to follow the person back on the social media venue they mentioned and perhaps start a collegial relationship. Who knows where that might lead?

Referrals

These days, almost all of my editing clients are either repeat customers or obtained through referrals. That is, Colleague A will hear that Company B is looking for an editor and will mention my name. Then either

Colleague A or Company B will get in touch with me and let me know about the opportunity, and I trot out the dog-and-pony show.

How do I get these referrals? I ask my friends and colleagues to let me know when they hear about projects that might suit me.

Just as important, I do the same thing for my colleagues, and I do it relentlessly. A client has a project I can't take on? I don't just say, "Sorry, no can do." I give them the name and contact information for someone who can. The next time that colleague hears about any opportunity that might suit me, you can bet they will pass it along. So give if you hope to get.

You don't have any writing friends or colleagues? You don't have any leads to pass along? You need to get hooked in, my friend. More on that in the networking section below.

Identify Who You're Going to Know

Earlier I mentioned that it's not who you know, it's who you get to know. If you were to make a plan to get to know some people who could help you succeed, who would you target? How would you go about meeting them?

Suppose you want to work with promising writers. You could join a bunch of writers' groups trying to meet them, or you could introduce yourself to a few agents and acquisitions editors and ask them to consider sending close-but-not-quite-there authors to you. I know several freelance editors who get a significant number of referrals from agents and acquisitions editors (to be clear, this is not that ethically questionable practice of agents/AEs getting kickbacks for referring authors to specific editors but rather agents and AEs having authors who ask for help and who keep lists of dev editors they trust and give out on request).

If you're looking for freelance work from publishing companies, identify a few targets and follow the staff editors who work there on social media. Do some non-stalkerish interaction with them. Then when your more formal letter of introduction (more on that in a moment) lands in their inbox, they will have some clue who you are and why they should read your email.

Direct and Indirect Marketing Approaches

Of course when I talk about getting to know people, I'm talking about networking, which gets a bad rap because of all those clueless idiots who do it wrong.

Networking is a form of indirect marketing. That is, you're not specifically selling a service to your potential client. You're saying, "Hey, let's get to know each other" not "Please book my editorial services."

In direct marketing, such as when you take out an ad, you *are* saying, "Book today!" Direct marketing tends to cost money whereas indirect marketing tends to cost time. Usually the best approach is to combine indirect and direct marketing efforts.

Networking

Networking, in the form that actually works, is not about schmoozing people and handing out your business card to anyone who will stand still long enough to take it. It's simply getting to know people. That's not so hard, is it?

Okay, on the scale of introversion, one through ten, you're an eleven, also you're an awkward and shy nerdish bookworm who sings random advertising jingles whenever they cross your mind, which is several times a day. (Ask me how I know.) Let me rephrase: It's hard but doable.

How can you get to know people?

My first suggestion is to join relevant professional organizations. They can help you grow your skills and understand your role as a freelancer. Organizations specifically meant for freelancers are good places to start.

Some of these organizations occasionally provide members with job leads, but, more important, you will learn a great deal from watching what your colleagues do (and interacting with them). The Editorial Freelancers Association is one of my favorites, but there are others.

Social media networking is a possibility. Follow potential clients (and mentors) on Twitter; join appropriate special interest groups on Facebook. The Editors' Association of Earth is a good one (**https://www.facebook.com/groups/EditorsofEarth**). And check out my group, Club Ed, as well (**https://www.facebook.com/groups/ClubEdGroup/**).

Join LinkedIn. Respond to some things other people are saying. Say a few things yourself.

Don't overcomplicate this process. People who do are completely missing the point. It's about connecting authentically with others, not about selling. The connecting comes first; the referrals will follow. However, don't be afraid to ask for help. An occasional, "Looking for a few editing clients" is absolutely fine. So is asking questions: "What has been your single most effective marketing strategy?"

Make contact with other editors, regardless of your area of specialization. One extremely busy technical editor constantly fends off requests for different types of nonfiction editing from the companies she works for. The few editors she knows personally get referrals from her all the time.

She's happy that she can help her companies out, the companies are happy because they can hire talented editors, and the editors are happy because they can get assignments without having to pound the pavement.

The more people you know in your field, the better you'll be able to sell your services. Networking is an essential but frequently overlooked part of successful freelancing.

Don't just network with the obvious people, like the editor-in-chief of a publishing company or indie writers who publish in the genres you edit. Think about who else works with your potential clients. Indie authors hire cover designers—say hello to a couple cover designers. A writing teacher might get asked for names of good editors—start a conversation.

Think strategically but make sure your interactions are authentic. You should be interested in what the writing teacher has to say. If you're not, move along and find someone else to connect with.

Another benefit of professional networking: forming friendships with other freelancers who can review project quotes, queries, and revision letters before you send them. This is a huge help and a favor you can return.

Position Yourself as an Expert

Getting interviewed as an expert is a good way to establish your credentials. If you're seen as an expert in your field, you can attract more business. Plus, clients believe editorial ("We interviewed Jane Doe, an expert in line-editing fiction . . .") more than they believe marketing ("Hire me! I'm great!")

You can be interviewed on podcasts and for print and online stories and blogs. Help a Reporter Out (www.helpareporter.com) and PR Leads (www.prleads.com) are businesses that connect journalists with experts, you being the expert. (I've used both.)

Pitching broadcast media (radio and television) is a more specialized skill (and there's tons of competition) so start by pitching yourself as a guest for podcasts and webinars, preferably those that target your potential clients. After you build confidence and gain experience you can go after bigger scores.

Learn how to pitch yourself as an expert—briefly explaining your credentials and why you're the person who can answer the interviewer's questions. Don't try to force your expertise to fit a stated need. If the request is: "Looking for thirty-something self-made millionaires" then don't respond with, "I'm fifty and I only have a hundred grand but I'm happy to talk!"

If you're not the right person this time, don't worry. Maybe you will be the next time.

Building your reputation is an indirect way to get clients, so you have to balance it with more direct efforts. In other words, don't spend all your time trying to get on *Good Morning, America,* while ignoring the email from your former boss asking for a quote.

Conduct Classes

Another way you can build your expertise (and get paid!) is by teaching classes. Such classes can be offered either at the college level or in a continuing education program. Arts organizations and professional associations sponsor classes. Or, you can develop your own self-sponsored classes and offer them online, using a learning management system like Moodle or Teachable. Or you can keep it even simpler and use Facebook groups or the Slack app for discussions.

Classes on creative writing, memoir writing, and similar pursuits are often well-received. Often you don't have to have any particular credentials to teach them except a willingness to talk about the subject matter in an authoritative way. The students in such classes could eventually become clients of your editing business.

While you can't spend the entire class period singing your own praises, you can let people know what you do for a living and give them access to your marketing materials. I always include a way for students to network with each other (and me).

Press Releases

Each time you accomplish something of interest, such as when you open for business or win any kind of industry award or praise, send a press release to the local media with information on what your business does and how people can contact you. Send your press release to the features editor (Google for an actual name — don't send a press release to a job title).

A good way to get local and regional press is to tie press releases to newsworthy or seasonal events to give them a sense of timeliness. Offer tips that show your expertise. For example, every November is National Novel Writing Month, and you might pitch your local paper or blog a press release with ten tips for what to do with the novel you finished during NaNoWriMo.

This is one of the cheapest, easiest ways to generate favorable local attention. You can send press releases to news publications throughout the country, but it will be harder to get their attention. (Local citizens tend to be of interest to local newspapers).

Press releases can also go to your alumni magazine or newsletter, a hometown newspaper, and trade magazines. Professional and trade associations you belong to can also be notified; they often list member achievements in their promotional materials. Local radio stations can also receive your press release. Target those that have interviews or talk show segments.

Write Articles

You can also generate inexpensive publicity and build your expertise by writing articles meant for fellow editors or for your potential clients (writers). In most cases, you pitch the article idea to the blog or magazine editor first and then if they like your idea they will assign you to write it.

If your article is published, you can add a tag (byline) stating who you are and what you do. (You might even get paid!)

You can start your own blog, but this can be a huge undertaking. It might be more efficient to guest post on other people's blogs. (More on starting your own blog below.)

Advertise Your Services

Advertising is simple enough: you pay to put your information in front of potential clients. I've been a freelancer for so long, I can remember when editors took out ads in the Yellow Pages. No one does that anymore but paid advertisements can still work as a way to drum up business. Do your research before spending money and test your results carefully. A Facebook ad may cost only ten dollars but if it doesn't get you anywhere, you'd have been better off spending that ten dollars on a nice box of tea.

Be cautious about advertising on the radio and television. I have never yet heard of an editor for whom this was a successful tactic. Better: get *interviewed* on radio or television as an expert (I talked about that earlier.)

Some freelance editors advertise in the periodicals produced by writers' organizations. If you want to give this a try, identify the right organization—for example, if you plan to edit romance, you'd want to advertise in the Romance Writers of America's monthly *RWA Report*. If you want to focus on mystery/thriller, you could approach the International Thriller Writers organization to advertise in their email newsletter. Any kind of custom publication or trade magazine that targets your potential clients could work.

Of course, advertising requires an upfront investment of cash with no guarantee of reward, but you may find it worthwhile to give it a try.

Add Your Profile to Job Directories

This is not something I do personally, but countless editors swear by it. Many membership organizations have directories where interested parties can find out more about hiring their members.

A potential client looking for, say, someone with experience editing computer manuals can look up a few key words and identify potential editors (this is different from job boards or job listings where the organization lists information about potential projects and you reach out to the client—in this case, the client reaches out to you).

Some matchmaking companies create databases of freelancers, then solicit clients to hire the company to provide the freelancers. The matchmaker gets a percentage of what the project is worth. Think Reedsy and Upwork.

Much of the work available at these places pays poorly but you can occasionally find good opportunities. For a newer editor, they can be one way to get your foot in the door and gain that all-important experience.

Send Letters of Introduction

Direct contact is simply reaching out to people who hire freelancers and asking them to hire you. The direct contact approach is the one most likely to freak out editors hoping to establish freelance careers. But unless you already know a lot of people who hire editors, it's going to be the best way to see immediate results.

Unlike a used car salesman, I'm not advocating the cold call—calling up people you don't know to solicit sales from them. In fact, it's probably best if you don't, at least not until after you've already made initial contact.

How do you make that initial contact? By sending a letter of introduction (LOI), usually by email (not spam!) to select people you'd like to do business with. How do you figure out who these prospects are? You just have to ask, "Who hires people who do the work I do?"

For me, when I first started out, the answer to that question was, "Book publishers." When I began freelance editing, it was after I'd written a few books and earned my PhD in English—those were my credentials. I didn't (maybe I shouldn't admit this) even really understand what CMOS was and why it mattered.

Armed with only these few and not directly relevant credentials, I sent out letters (this was back when people still did everything the old-fashioned way) to small and midsize publishing companies listed in *Writer's Market*.

I reasoned that these smaller companies would have only a few staff editors and that they'd have more work than they could reasonably do.

My logic was sound. Right away, I was hired for several different projects. Now that I had even more solid credentials, I sent out another series of letters to more publishers, and got more work.

Since that time, I have only occasionally used direct contact to find work, as nearly all of my clients come by referral or networking. However, newer colleagues attest to the power of the LOI. It still works.

Where to Send LOIs

Suppose you're willing to try sending out LOIs to people who you don't even know. Where would you find people to pitch? The answer, my friend, is all around!

Look at your bookshelves/Kindle. Who publishes the books you like to read? You could send a letter of introduction. To whom would you send it? The editor-in-chief is a good prospect. A senior developmental editor may hire for these positions. A copy chief usually handles copyediting freelancers (but not always). Also, don't forget that you can pick up the phone. Ask the receptionist where to send your information. When I've done this, I've never gotten a brush-off, although I know it's possible. If that happens, it won't kill you, I promise. Just call the next place on your list.

Often, publishers' websites (particularly those for ebook publishers) will have a career/jobs tab that shows whether they're currently hiring freelance editors. Become familiar with the different publishers in your area(s) of interest and make it a practice to regularly check their needs.

Your network of colleagues can help. Just ask.

So can Google, Publisher's Weekly (especially the "Deals" information), and LinkedIn.

I used *Writer's Market* to find my first editing jobs. There are now many resources available online that can help you track down publishing companies that can use your services.

Check out job boards, such as **www.edit2010.com** and **www.journalismjobs.com**. The members-only sections of **www.MediaBistro.com** and other freelance organizations also have job boards. I found a fantastic DE job with a publisher on JournalismJobs — one that has lasted many years. I still get projects from this contact! I also once found a worthwhile job on Craigslist.

Hang out with writers and editors and keep your eyes and ears open. One of my favorite hanging-out places when I first started doing this work was **www.FreelanceSuccess.com**. Though it has no job board, I heard about many opportunities through my colleagues there.

Follow publishers and editors on Twitter and find out about their needs that way.

Subscribe to newsletters (like Freelance Success, which I mentioned above) that profile markets. I landed a Barnes and Noble editing gig this way.

LOIs and Indie Authors

If you send out marketing emails to a bunch of indie authors who didn't ask for them, they'll probably perceive your efforts as spam, hit the delete button, and report you to the authorities. Contact with authors needs to be experienced as less intrusive than that to be effective.

A former colleague has a favorite way to form new relationships and put her editing business out there — she'll locate an author who is self-publishing and she'll send a quick email that says, basically, "I read about your novel on your website. Sounds fun!" Then she'll slowly build a relationship: by sending an e-mail message with an interesting statistic she ran across, by dropping an interesting article in the mail, by sending a personal note.

She never comes right out and says, "We should work together." Sometimes they never do work together, but the author often ends up being part of her network.

In general, though, if you don't finesse this, you'll be slammed for spamming people, so it might be better to follow indie authors on Twitter and to interact with their Facebook author pages.

You can use a newsletter that people have chosen to receive as a way to market directly to indie authors (more on that next).

Connect Using a Newsletter and/or Blog

Sending a regular newsletter can be a good way to keep in touch with potential, current, and former clients, but don't add people to your email list without getting their permission first.

One way to encourage people to sign up for your newsletter is to offer a premium in exchange for a newsletter signup. This is a freebie that will be attractive to your market, but which isn't marketing material, such as a report on ways to fix three common beginner mistakes in fiction (instead of "Why you should hire me to edit your book.")

Be aware that the European Union requires businesses to adhere to the General Data Protection Regulation (GDRP), so if any part of your audience is from the EU, you will want to be sure you understand best practices (for example, the use of premiums to get newsletter signups is addressed in the regulation).

Automating this process is the best way to make sure you don't run afoul of rules and laws and get suspended by your ISP or smacked with a fine. I use, and like, **www.Mailchimp.com**, but there are other email list management companies that can do the job for you.

Some editors also keep a blog on their website and update it frequently with tips for potential clients. One way to multiply the usefulness of your blog is to link it to your newsletter—write a blog post, then include the first paragraph and a link to the rest in your newsletter. You only have to write one article and it can serve several purposes for you.

Blogs can be tough to maintain and draw attention to, and they may not even convert readers into clients, but a newsletter list can be a very valuable marketing tool. Don't assume that you have to have a blog just because other people do, but if you do decide to keep a blog, try to maintain a regular posting schedule so that readers always know when to expect new material from you.

The freebie/premium, newsletter, and/or blog posts can help establish your expertise as an editor.

Help Wanted Ads

One way to use ads to build your business is to respond to them! Some freelancers have good success responding to help wanted ads. They introduce themselves to companies advertising for editorial help. They let these companies know that they can do the work freelance.

Often a company will choose to go this route instead of gambling on hiring a full-time staffer. A company can always "fire" a business that doesn't work out, but it's harder to do the same with an employee. If the business doesn't have to be trained the same way an employee would, so much the better. When the labor market is tight, freelancers provide an excellent alternative to letting a position remain unfilled for months on end.

Check online job boards and relevant trade magazines for ads that seek help you can provide on a freelance basis. Visit the websites of companies you might be able to do freelance work for, check out their employment listings, and send them your relevant marketing information.

Letter of Introduction

Once you've identified potential clients, you can send them a letter explaining who you are and how you might be able to help them. Below are a few sample letters of introduction (LOI) that you can use to give you ideas about how to write your own.

Letter in Response to Job Posting

I use a version of this letter to respond to postings about freelance openings, customizing it with particulars that relate to the desired qualifications.

Dear TWIMC*:

I'm writing in response to your job listing on JOB BOARD.** I'd love to be considered for the position of JOB I'M QUALIFIED FOR. As you can see from my attached resume, I've worked for many years as a freelance editor for book and magazine publishers. Functions I've fulfilled have included everything from substantive developmental editing to copyediting according to house style.

For nearly five years, I worked extensively with freelancers as editor of CUSTOM NICHE magazine, which also required me to work with all members of the production team to ensure a product that satisfied the client and made it to the printer on time, every time. More recently, I worked as JOB TITLE of PUBLISHING

COMPANY, which required me to acquire more than 200 books a year, many of which I also edited.

Currently, I teach developmental editing for ORGANIZATION, where in addition to teaching students the basics of developmental editing, I show them how to manage editor-author relationships, how to effectively write and resolve editorial queries, and how to tackle whatever manuscript problems arise — skills that I have learned myself over the years.

I'm also a writer with numerous book credits, including coauthorship situations that required playing well with others. I have taught an online classes in writing and editing for many years. I can provide references from writers whose books have made it through publication with my help.

I would be more than happy to answer questions about my background and experience.

All best,
Jennifer Lawler

*TWIMC = To Whom It May Concern. I use the person's name here.

**The job listing will specify various things the client is looking for — in this case, the ability to work well with writers, past book editing experience, etc. Tailor this letter to their needs. For a different listing, I would tweak the letter accordingly.

General Letter of Introduction

This is a version of a letter I use just to let people know about me (that is, I'm not writing in response to a job ad but am just sending out feelers). I will tweak this one depending on the type of publisher I'm approaching.

Dear TWIMC:

If that stack of manuscripts on your desk is threatening to topple over and bury you, you probably need some help. Let me take some of that work off your hands.

I'm an experienced developmental editor who can also provide copyediting services—for years I taught copyediting classes for ORGANIZATION, so I do know where all the commas go. Plus, I sleep with the Chicago Manual of Style.

I have worked as a freelance developmental editor for many book publishers, including NAME DROPPING GOES HERE, among others.

I'm also the author or coauthor of more than thirty books, so I know exactly how writers feel when they get that revision letter. I'm always careful to be polite, diplomatic, and encouraging in my communications with writers.

If you'd be interested in hearing more about how I may be able to help you, please drop me a line or give me a call. I can be reached at [contact information].

Thank you for your time.

All best,
Jennifer Lawler

Create a Landing Site

Once you've decided on your purpose, the kind of clients you'll market to, and have developed a basic plan for marketing your services, you need to tell the world. That begins with having a central location where clients can find out more about you.

"A central location where potential clients can find out more about you" is a website. It doesn't need to be fancy and it should be something you can easily update without going to a lot of expense. Your business is likely to evolve, especially in the first few years as you find your footing. It should be professional, but you don't have to invest thousands of dollars and hundreds of hours into designing and producing it. It should be mobile friendly since many people use their phones more than they do their computers.

You don't need to worry about SEO and trying to get your website to show up on the first page of results when people search for "Editor." That's not how you're going to get clients (a person searching for "editor" is the target market for people selling hundred-dollar edits. They're not one of your potential clients.)

Your website isn't about getting people who don't know who you are to find you. It's about giving people who've heard of you a place to find out more.

The website will not, of itself, generate clients, but it is the landing page for them—the way for them to check you out once they've heard of you. So you need to include the information that they'll need to know—who you are, what you do, possibly your rates, and your contact information. Make it easy for a potential client to connect with you.

It should include testimonials. Ask a former client or two if they could supply a few kind words about you. If you've received praise about your work, perhaps in an email responding to a project you did, ask if you can use a specific quotation from it. If you're just starting out and don't have clients, then ask people for whom you've done volunteer work, or, if you've done editing as an employee, use your former employer as a testimonial. If you've burned that bridge, well, you can always add testimonials later.

Your website doesn't have to include a blog if that is not part of your marketing strategy.

A Facebook page is not a website. It can be a useful supplement, and a handy place for Facebookers to find out more about you, but remember that not everyone is on Facebook, that Facebook pages are hard to promote without paying money to do so, and that you don't own a Facebook page, so Facebook can decide to do whatever they want with that audience you spent months building.

It's always better to control at least some of the means of production.

Chapter 3

Client and Project Management

After you've acquired the necessary editing skills and done some marketing, at some you point you will get a client. Yay, you! While it may feel like landing the client already took a lot of work, now you actually have to do the work you were hired to do. And not only that, you have to do it in a way that makes your client happy. This keeps your invoices paid, referrals coming in, and clients returning for more.

Fundamentals of Client Management

Excellent customer service keeps clients returning to you on a regular basis. We all know the basics of good customer service because we've all been customers. Rude clerks can make you vow never to return to a certain department store. Nothing can get you steamed quite so quickly as a receptionist finishing a ten-minute personal phone call before asking you who your appointment is with. Long lines at a checkout can be irritating, especially if employees are doing other tasks instead of helping out. Contractors who promise to have the plumbing fixed by this Friday but don't bother showing up until a week from Tuesday can try the patience of the gentlest souls.

As customers, we know what good customer service is:

- being acknowledged and welcomed pleasantly and promptly
- having someone listen courteously to a complaint
- provider does the work as promised and meets deadlines
- project completed on budget or overruns are clearly explained and approvals sought ahead of time

In our practice, following the items on this list means responding politely and promptly to inquiries about our services (even when we're busy or doubt the inquirer is a good match), listening attentively and respectfully to criticism and feedback (even when we don't agree with it), and doing the work as agreed to, (even when we experience some bumps along the way).

In the day-to-day world of real business, good customer service can sometimes be a challenge to deliver. Sometimes different clients have competing needs, or you make a mistake, or the client makes a mistake. Preventing situations like these from turning into disasters requires communicating effectively with your clients.

Since the ability to manage and negotiate client expectations is the key to success, the phrase "client management" is probably more accurate than "customer service" when it applies to our businesses.

You Set the Rules

Often new freelancers are so intent on getting their first few clients that they forget the golden rule of freelancing: Just because someone wishes to hire you, you are under no obligation to provide the service.

One common iteration of this is when the client doesn't have a reasonable budget. They're thinking $100 and you're thinking $1000. You don't need to try to find a way to make this work or even to have a discussion about it, although if you can offer a lesser service for a lesser price, that may be worth a try.

By the same token, you don't have to edit mss with content you object to. You don't have to work with people you object to. You don't have accept payment in forms you object to. You get to decide. Now, obviously, the more open you are to content, people, and payment methods, the more likely you'll be a match with a client. But you're a freelancer now! You set the rules.

Clear Communication

The crucial thing is to *communicate* those rules. That starts with how you market. Everything from your advertising message to your website can help define the kinds of clients you want to attract and should communicate what it's like to work with you.

Are you rigorous and demanding or gentle and handholding (or some combination thereof)? Do you accept only Bitcoin or mandrake root harvested under the first full moon of autumn? Make sure you clearly convey that information to your potential clients.

Sometimes freelancers feel a little hesitant about the business aspects of their work, such as asking for payment upfront, but in all my years of freelancing, none of my problems have come from saying, "I charge $X for that and expect payment in full before I begin." They have all come from not clearly explaining my expectations or not understanding the client's expectations.

Different Clients, Different Needs

Good client management means understanding that every potential client is different. For this reason, I recommend using caution when making across-the-board promises and guarantees. Instead of including a banner on your website that promises you'll turn around edits within two weeks, give a range, such as two to six weeks, depending on how large the project is and how busy you are.

People would rather have a realistic expectation than be given a specific promise you can't keep. You can nail down a specific deadline with the client once you have a clearer sense of what the project will entail and when it will need to be scheduled.

If you're already booked for the next six months, say so immediately so that a potential client can adjust her expectations. Some editors announce on their websites,

"Scheduling for June" or whatever is true in order to create realistic expectations.

It's crucial not to make assumptions about any one client. Some authors are so fragile that one even moderately critical comment will undo them. (You might not find the comment, "All of the characters have one-syllable names starting with M, which could be confusing to the reader, so consider changing a few of these names" to be cruelly stated but there is at least one author who found it so.) Yet others want you to tell them directly and without sugarcoating exactly where they're going wrong so they can take the necessary measures. You don't know until you've had at least some preliminary interaction with the author.

Develop Trust

Trust is the basis of all good relationships, including business relationships. Clients need to trust that you'll be competent and deliver on what you've agreed to. Building trust requires attention to details: meeting deadlines, being reasonably available to answer emails and calls (not 24/7, that's insane), and letting clients know when you'll be unavailable. Often it's little things, like your missing a scheduled call, that can make or break a business relationship. Just like any relationship, clients want to know you're invested in making it a success, too.

In order to build trust with your clients, be open and honest about any problems and concerns. Do what you say you're going to do and admit it if you can't. A client would much rather know a week beforehand that you'll be late with the edit because you broke your hand in a freak curling accident than to find this out two hours after the edit is due.

And while you don't have any control over whether your clients will do what they're supposed to do, setting a good example by meeting all of your agreements makes it harder for clients to rationalize their own bad behavior. If you go silent for a month during a project despite the client's request for an update, you can't be terribly surprised when the client goes quiet for a month after you submit your invoice.

Here again, setting expectations is key. When my daughter was young and in and out of hospitals a lot, I didn't bill myself as the quick-turnaround freelancer. If you were in a hurry, I was not your go-to person. I couldn't make those kinds of promises—I never knew when we'd end up in the ER again. So, I focused on the longer-term projects where an email returned tomorrow instead of today didn't create a migraine for anyone. Most people I worked with never realized anything unusual about my personal situation.

It may be that your situation is different—maybe you never know where you're going to be in six months, so you never book much beyond the end of the month. That's fine. Book through the end of the month and add everyone else to a waitlist. All kinds of possibilities work, as long as you set expectations clearly.

Note: This is something I see a lot so it deserves a warning. One sure-fire way to lose trust is to mock clients on social media—even if you don't give any identifying information about the client or the project, no one wants to be a potential target. By the same token, don't make fun of basic mistakes. ("OMG! Info-dumping = amateur hour!") A lot of staff people do this (especially acquisitions editors and agents) so it's easy to fall into the trap, but gatekeepers can get away with this type of thing. You can't. (More trustworthy: "I see a lot of info-dumping when I edit. Here's how to avoid it . . . .") I always say that as a freelance editor, the only person you can poke fun at is yourself.

Giving Potential Clients the Brush-Off

Any freelancer with a website, an email address, and any kind of online presence is going to get inquiries from people who are not at all serious about shelling out real money for professional services. They just want to see what they can get for their hundred dollars.

These are not your potential clients and it is best to move them along. Over the years, I've found the easiest way to get them out of my hair is to send a boilerplate email: "Here's what I do and here's generally what it costs. Right now, I'm booking projects for MONTH. If you're interested, I'd love to hear more about your project. Send [whatever is appropriate to the inquiry — the genre and length, the first few chapters, etc.] and we can talk further."

The typical response is, "Oh, I'm not ready yet!" or "Oh, my budget won't stretch that far, sorry!" And that's fine. I'm not trying to convert everyone into a client. I am trying to find the potential clients who will be a good match, and this does it for me.

Note that sometimes you are not a match for reasons that have nothing to do with budget. Maybe the person who has approached you writes in a genre you don't edit or requires expertise you can't supply. Give a referral to another editor if you can. If not, just be honest: "I appreciate your thinking of me, but I don't edit mysteries and because of that I couldn't do your work justice." Or "I looked over your sample and feel you would do better with an editor who specializes in working with established authors. My editorial approach is more suitable for beginners." (Or vice versa, of course!)

The client will understand and won't be left wondering if his/her project was so awful you couldn't bear to look at it. (Remember that most authors grapple with serious self-doubt in those moments when they're not elated by their own brilliance.) The fact that you know your limits and understand that different genres and different skill levels require different editorial approaches does more to cement your expertise than does taking on projects you have no chance of successfully completing.

. . . Or Not

Some freelancers see a bite on the line as an opportunity to convert, so they spend time trying to engage potential clients in conversation in the hopes that they can squeeze more than a hundred dollars out of them. Such editors may have great success with that. If this is the approach you want to pursue, your boilerplate will be more about luring them in than sending them off.

For example, you might say something along the lines of, "My pricing is flexible depending on the project. Why don't we schedule a quick call (no charge!) and discuss it?"

Either way, even if you're sure you're not going to work with the potential client, be unfailingly polite. You can close the door on the two of you working together right now without setting any bridges on fire. This is not just because it's the decent thing to do but because you never know. Just because you think a project sounds hopeless doesn't mean the client is. Maybe the client will come around with a better project next time or maybe s/he will refer others to you. If you're dismissive, neither thing will happen.

Ask Questions

Newer freelancers are sometimes a little intimidated by their clients. A client approaches them, says, "I need this project by Y, I'll pay you X," and that's acceptable. Then, after the freelancer gets to work, she has some questions, but she's afraid to approach the client. She doesn't want to come across as less than professional or to seem like a pest. Those are legitimate concerns — but as long as you know how to edit and you're not pelting the client with emails every five minutes, then it's unlikely the client will perceive you as inexpert or pesky.

In other words, if you need to have certain information to do the job right, then you need that information. There's nothing wrong with asking questions.

If you can anticipate the kinds of questions you'll have, and if you'll pull them together so that the client is only answering one or two e-mails from you instead of ten, that's helpful. As you gain more experience, you'll know what types of questions you'll be likely to have, and can ask them in preliminary conversations about the project.

You may find that developing a template can help — checklists are so useful in freelancing! You don't necessarily show the template to the client, although some people do.

Setting Expectations
(for You and the Client)

Set and manage expectations by working out — *before* you begin an edit — all of the details of what will be done on the project. This means identifying and nailing down everyone's expectations, yours and the client's. This includes the scope of work, all deadlines (yours, the client's, and any other party's), the cost, and when payment is due.

Scope of Work

The scope of work is basically what you'll do and when. You must be sure you understand before you begin what is wanted and how it will be delivered to the client ("deliverables"). The scope of work becomes part of your project quote, the document you send to a client that details the work you will do and how much it will cost (project quotes are described more completely later in this chapter).

I've been asked to provide "line edits" to clients who have variously meant proofreading, copyediting, and developmental editing, so you can see why it's important to hammer out exactly what this means ahead of time.

Many freelancers include clear descriptions of each service they offer on their websites and ask clients to confirm their understanding of what they're looking for before going forward.

Sometimes a client will ask for one kind of service ("proofread my manuscript") when what they *need* is another kind of service (such as a developmental edit). I was recently asked to do what I would call a glorified copyedit (mostly line edits with some attention paid to organization and structure) on a manuscript that needed significant work on the concept level before it could succeed. I went back to the client with my assessment and the client agreed, so a different edit was arranged.

In another recent case, a client came to me for a bit of coaching to help her define her audience in order to develop a pitch letter but ended up asking me to edit the entire manuscript, a process that evolved as I asked questions about her project and process.

Providing a service is not like selling widgets. We can try to be standardized and straightforward ("Here's my menu of services and my fees"), but we also need to take into account the seemingly infinite variety of needs we may encounter. So don't be too wedded to one approach and don't be surprised or frustrated when people want you to customize your edit.

Mostly: communicate with the client. You can provide different levels of service depending on someone's budget and offer packages of services, depending on what clients are likely to need, but keep in mind that sometimes needs evolve. (Such as the above-referenced project that went from editing a pitch letter to editing a project.)

I recommend writing a project quote for any project of significant size. When accepted it serves as your agreement (though some freelance editors prefer to use contracts, which are covered in Chapter 7). If something will only take a few hours of my time I am less formal about the arrangement and will usually just invoice the client with a brief description of what I'm doing ("critique of revision letter"). I have a templated invoice I use for things like this.

Avoiding Scope Creep

"Sometimes needs evolve" is also called "scope creep" — where what you end up doing is far more than what you agreed to do in the first place. For instance, you agreed to do one round of developmental editing on a ms, and now the client wants weekly check-ins and a couple of brainstorming sessions while s/he is working on the revision, plus you won't mind reviewing the revision and letting him/her know if additional work is needed, will you?

Clients like this often not only expect you to fit all of this new work in at their convenience but don't understand why it should cost more since it can't possibly take that long to do.

I've had occasions where I've done one round of developmental edits, then find myself answering questions about the edit for (literally! this is not hyperbole!) the next three years. And there's that one client who keeps sending emails asking if I can "just take a peek at this and tell me what you think."

So, over the years, I've learned to be very specific about what "one round of developmental edits" means (it does include some support, but not unlimited and not forever).

I've also learned to set boundaries: "That was not in our original agreement but I can do it for $X." Often clients are willing to pay this additional fee with no problem, they just never actually pose the question that way. Instead of asking, "What would it cost for you to also review my revision and schedule coaching sessions for the next three weeks?" they will say, "Oh, when can you review my revision? And can you schedule a coaching session this week?"

The more you can visualize potential areas of scope creep, the easier it is for you to head it off. The more specific you are about the work you will do, the easier it is to draw a line: "This is beyond the scope of what we've agreed."

You can take a project approach: "Here's what's included in this package: One round of edits, up to three hours of email/phone coaching to answer questions about the revision process, a review of the author's revision for errors that might have crept in, and a final set of edits to reconcile any outstanding problems."

Or you can do it a la carte: "Here's what one round of edits cost. Here is what email/phone coaching costs. Here is what a review of the author's revision costs."

Your best approach may be something a little different from either of these versions. What you don't want to happen is to earn an effective hourly rate of three dollars. Clearly defining your boundaries can help prevent that.

When you deliver the, ah, deliverables, reiterate the agreement: "Here's the edit I promised by the the time I promised it. I will provide Specific Additional Service once I have your revisions/get your final payment/etc., which we agreed you would send me by Deadline."

This keeps the details of your agreement front and center and allows for any necessary additional discussion to occur before the project goes off the rails.

Note that you should also say, "Invoice attached" (if any payment is due) and attach it. The client may ask you to submit invoices in some other way, such as a cranky web interface designed to make you abandon all hope of payment, but including it with your delivery email serves as an additional reminder that you're not doing this work because it's so good for your heart health.

Negotiation

We'll discuss the nitty-gritty of setting rates and talking money with clients in Chapter 5, but negotiation is an important part of client management, so I'm discussing it in this chapter.

Defining expectations is a process of negotiation. People often think of negotiation as something that only applies to the fee. It's not. All aspects of a project—deadline, deliverables, fees—are subject to negotiation. Don't forget that changing the deadline or the deliverables can trigger higher or lower fees, if you want. If a client needs an edit done in a rush, you can charge a rush fee to do it. Or you may be willing to discount your fee a bit if they'll give you more time to do it, or if they have several projects at a time for you.

Although some of your clients will either accept or decline your quote without fuss, some will wish to negotiate. There's nothing wrong with this! Some freelancers feel that negotiations indicate conflict or a potentially difficult client but that's not the case.

Basics of Negotiation

Think of clients who want to negotiate as people who are trying to tell you what's important to them. If you listen, you can end up with a new client and a nice deposit in your bank account.

Suppose you say, "I charge sixty dollars an hour. For the job you've described, I anticipate it would take ten hours." If the client says, "Ten hours?" that's not a sign that you must immediately back down—or even a sign that you need to explain yourself. It's not even (necessarily) a red flag. You're the expert. You know how long it will take, so remain firm. When the client says, "At sixty dollars an hour?" and appears to be thinking about taking the job elsewhere, you still stand firm.

If the client says, "That's too much," do not—I repeat, do not—say, "Okay, how about thirty dollars an hour?" (By the same token, don't say, "Buh-bye" either, unless you have so much business you are trying to get potential clients to stop bothering you.)

In this situation, you can negotiate. Negotiating does not mean you drop your rate. It means the client gives up something and you give up something. It's that simple.

So your next question might be, "What's your budget?" People don't like to give this information but once you've offered a starting point, it's usually easier to get them to open up. If the client says, "I was thinking a hundred dollars tops for the whole project," then you are so far apart that all the good faith in the world will not find a common ground, so *now* you can say "Buh-bye!"

If the client says, "I was thinking closer to five hundred, not six hundred," then you've got some room to maneuver. But, again, don't just say, "Okay, I'll do it for five hundred." The client needs to give something up for this to be a negotiation and not just you caving to pressure.

You can say, "I offer a five percent discount for full payment in advance" if you don't already expect payment in full in advance. Or you can say, "I can do a less complete service that doesn't include a coaching phone call for less money and this might still suit your needs and would fit your budget." (Or whatever is a lesser service you can offer.)

It's Not Just the Money

By the way, the above example is one reason why I prefer to quote a fee for the whole project rather than sharing my hourly rate and my estimate of how many hours it will take — if the client can't see why it should take ten hours, then that becomes another pain point in the negotiation process. However, in some cases, such as when I'm coaching clients, hourly is the only realistic way to go.

Maybe the fee is fine but the client balks at paying half or all of it ahead of time. You might say, "I can charge in three installments, but I do add a ten percent administrative fee for that."

Or maybe you can offer a discount if the client agrees to give you more time to do the project, or refers a friend to you or whatever could work. Often just listening to the client allows the client to talk himself/herself into it: "You know what, it's not that big a deal. Let's do the project as you quoted and that'll be fine."

The Project Quote

After a potential client has come to you and you've reviewed the manuscript to be edited, you will need to deliver a project quote. This is a description of what you will do, when you will do it by, and how much it will cost.

Here's an example with explanation:

Dear Potential Client:

Thank you for thinking of me to edit your novel! I've had a chance to take a peek at your manuscript (1), *Love Lies Bleeding on the Ground*. I would be happy to provide a complete developmental edit on this manuscript. Please note that the following quote refers to the full manuscript of 80,535 words that you sent on October 1. I can't promise the quote will stay the same if the ms has changed (2).

As we discussed, you want me to identify problems with the narrative arc, such as plot holes and threads that aren't tied up, as well as to provide suggestions for creating a more believable character arc for the protagonist. In addition, I will look for related developmental problems, such as scenes that contain unnecessary exposition, a central conflict that could be sharpened, and concerns with world-building/setting (3).

This edit will include queries and limited line edits on the manuscript itself to help you see where the problems are cropping up and how to fix them, plus a five-to-seven page revision letter that will provide a plan for your revision (4). It does not include copyediting, although I will correct egregious errors that I spot.

The edit includes up to three hours of email/phone coaching to answer questions about the edit and to support your revision process. Any time required beyond these three hours is billed at my hourly rate of $X an hour (5).

As we further discussed, I will review your revision and make a final set of edits to reconcile any outstanding problems (see dates below) (6).

My fee for providing this service is $X. If you would like to book this edit, my next available opening is DATE. I will need your 25 percent nonrefundable deposit of $Y by A FEW DAYS FROM NOW (7) to hold this time for you. I will return my first round of edits to you by ABOVE DATE PLUS HOW MANY WEEKS IT WILL TAKE TO DO THE EDIT (8). Final payment will be due at this time (9). You will need to return your revision to me for my review and final edits by DATE PLUS TWO MONTHS. If you do not return your revision to me by the deadline, I will not be able to provide the final review (10).

Please remember that the deposit is nonrefundable. If you cancel the edit ahead of time, I cannot return your deposit as I cannot guarantee that your spot will be taken by someone else (11).

Once you've agreed to the quote, I'll send you an invoice for the deposit (12).

Thank you very much! I look forward to hearing from you.

Sincerely,
Smart Editor

(1) I never suggest that I have done any serious examination of the ms because then the author will want to know what is wrong with it before I've even done the edit.

(2) Authors are notorious for saying, "Wait, wait, read this version!" I can't promise that my assessment of "Oh, this is in fairly good shape" will remain the same if the author takes it into his/her head to completely start over.

(3) This paragraph describes what the edit—in this case a developmental edit—will include. It's notable for what it isn't: looking for incorrect comma placement and other sundries.

(4) This paragraph defines the deliverables—what the author can expect to receive.

(5) This paragraph defines what happens when the allotted coaching time is exceeded. It's a good reminder that the author can pay for additional time if wanted.

(6) If any part of the process requires the client to take action, be sure to define what that action is and when it must be taken by.

(7) The amount of the deposit can vary—maybe it's one-third or one-half or maybe it's a dollar amount (I require full payment in advance)—whatever it is, make it clear that it's yours once the client books the edit with you.

(8) Just as you want the author to commit to a deadline, you need to commit to a deadline!

(9) Always, always, always make it clear when the final payment is due.

(10) Again, this confirms #6—any necessary action the client must take and when the client must take it by. Note that it includes the consequences if the client does not.

(11) This section is for any policies you have to prevent cancelations and no-shows.

(12) You can instead use a link to an online booking form or a Paypal button to pay the deposit—just make sure it's clear what the author needs to do to pay the deposit.

Use a template for your project quote to make sure you don't overlook anything important.

Preventing and Dealing with Problem Clients

A clearly written project quote can help prevent misunderstandings and keep potential problems from torpedoing an edit. But sometimes not even the most detailed agreement can head off disaster. So, here are some recommendations for preventing and dealing with problem clients.

No-Shows, Cancelations, and the Disappearing Final Payment

You'll see that the above model project quote includes a penalty for canceling an edit. If you don't make it clear that the client is booking a particular slot on your schedule, and that it can't be moved around at will, clients will expect you to accommodate them.

This is especially true if you book clients before they've finished writing the ms. A lot of editors do this, especially for repeat clients, but it supposes the author won't have any of the problems authors often have when completing a ms—busy time at the day job, trouble solving a plot issue that slows down their progress, false start on the story that requires significant rewriting, etc. These are the typical problems that will result in an author wanting to cancel or reschedule an edit.

Some Preventative Measures

I don't accept bookings from indie authors until their mss are complete, which means I don't have a problem with cancelations — but much of my work is from publishers, so such a policy may not be realistic for people booking mostly or only indie authors.

In any case, you will need to be sure your clients understand the consequences of canceling or rescheduling. You may want to be more flexible — say, you only charge the deposit if they don't give you thirty days' notice or if you can't book another client into the vacated spot.

Sometimes clients are just no-shows. They booked an edit to start March 1, March 1 comes and goes, and nothing happens. You send a note on March 2, and still nothing. March 3, also nothing. You waste the week twiddling your thumbs. You've been ghosted!

You can't necessarily prevent this from happening. You can take some steps, such as emailing the client a reminder a few days ahead of time so that if something has come up — the client has lost his/her job and can't afford the edit — s/he might own up and tell you. This gives you a little time to see if you can move someone else into the now-open slot or otherwise reconfigure your schedule (and cash cushion!) to accommodate.

No matter what you do to prevent it, sometimes — even when everything seems right on target — the author's ms just never shows up. When this happens, make sure you don't book that client again. Do keep the deposit.

Useful Solutions to Consider

Keep a waitlist of potential clients for just such an emergency or offer a short-term deal to generate some income—for this week only, you'll review people's query letters for some reasonable fee.

Occasionally an author does not make the final payment. I avoid this by getting the entire fee upfront. Other people use different strategies. For example, you can watermark the ms in Word, then save it as a PDF and only share the "unlocked" version after you receive full payment. Other editors send first and last chapter to show the edit is complete but hold on to the middle section and the revision letter until final payment is received.

In general, I don't make policies like this until I have an actual problem—you may go twenty years without ever having a problem with a client not paying your final fee, so don't spend a lot of time and effort trying to solve problems that don't exist yet.

Potential Client Red Flags

Since we want to weed out potentially troublesome clients before they make our lives miserable, it's a good idea to have some weed-killing processes in place. For example, requiring a nonrefundable deposit means that people are more committed to the edit (and paying the final invoice) than if you don't require any upfront investment.

When you have what seems to be shaping up into a problem, be sure to check with editor groups and your colleagues to find out what you can do to either save the situation or keep from repeating it.

Here are some red flags I've discovered in my years of freelancing. Tread carefully if any of these crop up.

Being Asked to Work on Spec

Working on spec — "speculation" — means you aren't guaranteed anything for your work. You only get paid if the client decides to pay you after you're done. This is a big fat nope. If you're trying to build experience and credentials, at least arrange a barter in exchange for your efforts.

A related gambit is to suggest that you do the work for "exposure" — that is, the client will tell everyone about your work and you'll get lots of clients! Yeah, no. As the freelance saying goes, people die of exposure.

A variation of this is to promise lots of future work if you do *this* project inexpensively. It's true that some client relationships last for a long time and provide you with many projects over the years. But unless the client is booking all those projects right now, with deposits to match (in which case you might be willing to offer a small discount), it's best to take this one with a grain of salt.

The best long-term relationships begin as you would like them to continue: with the client valuing your work enough to pay you fairly for it.

Being Asked to Edit a Sample

It's not uncommon for someone to want you to edit a sample before hiring you. Now, I'm not against doing samples to help make sure you're the right person for the job. It can help seal the deal for copy editors, who are fixing sentence-level problems.

But this is tricky when we're talking about developmental editing because we don't necessarily know what the real issues are before we read the entire ms. It's easy to miss something if you're just glancing at the first few chapters.

Instead, show potential clients samples of work you've already done (with the original client's permission, of course). If you don't have anything you can share, then make something up as a sample. Or, go to the Gutenberg Project (**www.Gutenberg.org**) and download a novel that is out of copyright protection and edit a chapter or two of that as a sample.

If you do edit a sample of the client's work before booking them, as some editors do, make sure to keep the time spent on the project brief—no more than half an hour or so, which translates to a few pages at most. You can choose the pages if you want to prevent a potential client from trying to scam you.

More on edit tests for publishing company clients later in the chapter (these are not a red flag but a reality you will need to decide how you want to deal with).

Client Underestimates the Work Involved

Potential clients sometimes underestimate the work/skill involved in a project. This is often expressed when they say that a project should be easy or fast. This is a red flag for a number of reasons. Often, it means the client is devaluing your work ("How hard can it be to look for plot holes?") or doesn't understand what, exactly, you do ("You just use spell check, right?")

The work we do isn't just about the time we invest in it but our expertise as well—the knowledge and skill we bring to the table. A client who doesn't respect that is going to be a problem client.

Sometimes the client is just referring to logistical considerations—it's a short ten-thousand word novella, so of course the edit will go faster as compared to a complicated two-hundred-thousand-word tome that describes the history of the universe in mathematical terms. Or sometimes they want a simple process— someone to check for egregious errors, even if that means leaving in some less-than-perfect sentences.

Your job is to figure out which category the client falls into—the one who devalues your work or the one who is just using a shorthand method of referring to logistical considerations.

The Disappearing or Disorganized Client

Clients who wander off during the early stages of discussing their project are likely to wander off during the part of the project where they're supposed to do some work or, you know, pay you. If, during the onboarding process, they miss phone calls or don't respond to emails within a reasonable length of time, they're probably going to be painful to work with. Proceed with caution.

By the same token, clients who are disorganized during initial talks can quickly become time-consuming pits of need. It's fairly common for an author to say, "Oh, wait, don't use that version of the ms, use this one," but if they do this more than once in the early stages of discussion, tread cautiously (and it should go without saying that once you've started editing, they can't change drafts).

If the potential client can't seem to remember what you said in your previous email or seems to be mistaking you for one of the other editors they're thinking about using, treat the situation as if the red flags are waving because they are.

Client Continually Reopens Negotiations

Related to this is the client who wants to reopen negotiations once you've agreed to the basic parameters of the edit. It's one thing for a project to evolve, where, for example, you do an edit and then the author decides to purchase additional coaching. And negotiation is part of the process in the early stages: "I won't be able to revise the novel according to the deadline you have in the project quote—can we move that out a week?"

But it's another thing for agreed-upon details to be subject to re-negotiation: "I'm going to be a week late, okay?" after the edit has been scheduled or "My budget has changed, I won't be able to pay what we agreed for the edit" after you've begun the work. The client who wants to continually reopen negotiations is often one who is not committed to the process.

An earlier, more subtle signal is when the client has a lot of questions about the process: "What happens if I don't have my ms finished by the time the edit is scheduled? What happens if I decide to go with someone else after I pay the deposit? What if I don't like your work? What if I don't need any of the coaching you include in the package, can I get a refund on that?"

It isn't that clients shouldn't have questions. It's that the volume of questions suggests the client isn't ready to commit and doesn't feel confident in their decision. Often, maybe even most times, this has nothing to do with you. Point the author to your policies and let them know that booking with you is a firm commitment to you. Proceed knowing that this is a red flag.

Hesitating at the Down Payment

Related to the client who wants to re-open negotiations (because they're not committed) is the client who doesn't want to pay the down payment (also a clue that they're not committed). You'll hear this as "Can I book the slot but make the payment next week?" or variations on the theme. You may be tempted to accommodate because maybe they're just waiting for their paycheck and who hasn't had to do that. But the best policy is simply to say that you can only book the spot once you have the down payment. They can check back with you next week and see if the slot is still open then.

If you're not careful, you'll be holding this slot open for a month and then you'll hear, "Whoops, time got away from me, can you hold open NEW TIME for me?"

Until you finally retire, having never worked on their project.

The "Everyone Else Sucks" Client

It may feel warm and fuzzy to be the ONE editor who isn't a blithering idiot, but a client who has steamed through a lot of editors, none of whom has done a good job, is waving a red, red flag, and you should consider yourself warned.

Now, it does happen that some editors are incompetent, and when a client finds this out, s/he gets mad and goes in search of a new editor. And it sometimes happens that the client has had a couple of unsatisfactory experiences, and this is, in fact, because the editors don't know what they're doing. In some cases, the only one at fault is the editor(s).

But we're not talking about rocket science, so having a slew of unsatisfactory business dealings with editors is at some point more about the client than the editors. Even if all of them are incompetent, where is s/he finding them in the first place and why is s/he making the same hiring mistakes over and over?

Often, the problem isn't in the editor(s) but in the client, who doesn't know what s/he wants, doesn't understand the editorial process, doesn't know what an editor does or doesn't do, and is unwilling to learn.

Yes, you can see where that might be a problem.

In this case, I recommend scheduling a quick phone call before going too far with the client. This will be a quick and fairly straightforward way of figuring out whether the client merely had a run of bad luck or is a run of bad luck.

Special Considerations with Publisher Clients

If you're targeting publishing companies or book packagers as potential clients, be aware that this process has its idiosyncrasies.

Edit Tests

If you connect with a publisher who is looking for a freelance editor (whether CE, DE, or proofreader), you will almost certainly be asked to take an editing test, or possibly a series of editing tests. It's not required across the board—I've been hired without having to take a test. But on other occasions, I've needed to pass one (particularly in circumstances where the publisher is looking for someone to take on a long-term workload versus an editor who has gotten behind and just needs someone to take one manuscript off her hands).

You will need to know to expect this, and to decide what to do about it. Some freelancers feel their experience should preclude their having to do an editing test and refuse them. That's certainly understandable, but in some cases you simply won't be hired without taking the test.

For proofreaders, you might be asked to compare the typeset draft of a ms with the copyedited version to make sure the correct changes were made. Or you might be asked to review the final ms and catch any egregious errors before the book is published.

For CE, you'll be asked to review a chapter from a book (or something similar), given a little information about the project, such as a CE memo, and expected to edit the material (line edits/queries) according to the house style.

For DE, you may be asked to provide line edits as well as to write a revision letter outlining your overall developmental concerns. Often, in addition to showing your DE chops, you'll need to show that you understand the basics of copyediting (that you know how to use a style guide, that you understand how to untangle a confusing sentence).

Just be sure that you understand what the client wants you to do on the test and follow the instructions.

Scam Alert!

Be aware that some people (not legitimate publishers) use "tests" to scam editorial services from editors. They'll ask ten different people to do a free "sample" edit on ten different chapters of their book, then think they'll be able to revise their work without having to pay anyone to edit the whole thing. Of course, you can imagine how ridiculous that revision is going to end up being, but the scam artist doesn't know this.

So, use caution when responding to postings on Craigslist and similar places. Just because the scammer is using some real-sounding company name doesn't mean they're not a scammer.

Hiring Expectations

Also, be aware that even legitimate publishers can have ridiculous expectations of freelancers. We're not applying to be staffers but sometimes they act as if we are. Just be proactive about finding out what their process is. If being considered for freelance projects requires five rounds of interviews and a trip to a city three thousand miles from home, maybe it's an opportunity to pass up. The key is to find out ahead of time what their decision-making process will entail. Then you can decide if you want to be part of it.

Identifying Customer Service Problems

If potential clients repeatedly turn down your project quotes or if clients never hire you again after the first project, you should investigate what's going wrong. Although acquiring a variety of clients is a good idea — in general, you don't want one client making up more than twenty-five percent of your business so that if the work dries up/client goes out of business/your contact finds another job, you won't be standing in the middle of a disaster — you also want to hang on to the clients you already have.

The clients you lose can tell you a lot about how you run your company and how you can improve it. But asking your *satisfied* customers to rate your customer service skills ranks among the more useless undertakings. You don't necessarily need to know why you have clients; you need to know why you don't.

You need to find out what makes a customer quit working with you or refuse to work with you to begin with.

Pick Up the Phone

All you have to do is call. I know — who am I kidding, right? But I'm serious. You have to ask. Don't take the answers personally. It's just business. "We want someone with five years' experience" when you only have three is not a personal rejection.

Ask clients you've worked for once and who never hired you again if they would be willing to share why your services didn't meet their needs. And if you've worked with potential clients who ultimately decided to go with someone else, ask if they would mind telling you why.

Perhaps your materials seem unpolished or amateurish. Perhaps you don't work quickly enough or else you promised deadlines that you didn't meet. Perhaps your rates are too high or the client suddenly developed an aversion to six-foot blondes. (Notice that some of these things are not like the others.)

Responding to Feedback

I'm not saying you need to change the way you operate your business on the basis of one dissatisfied client's comments. Maybe someone felt your rates were too high. This doesn't mean you should start charging less. It simply means that your rates were too high for that company/person. If this complaint is echoed by other dissatisfied clients or if you have trouble acquiring clients, however, you may need to pay more serious attention to the question of rates.

Potential clients who decided not to hire you might say you had a misspelling on your website, which calls your credibility as an editor into question. Or there's a glitch in how your portfolio loads or the Paypal button doesn't work. (You can also ask friends to walk through any technology you use—can they easily access a booking page and pay the deposit, or does something stop them from navigating your site easily?) These are things you can easily fix.

Sometimes the answer will have nothing to do with your skills. Perhaps a publishing company began doing all their formerly freelance work in-house. You can't do much about that decision except occasionally remind the client that you'd be happy to help them out should they need extra assistance on a special project. When you're not to blame, the reasons for your clients' defections often seem unfair.

You don't always have control over what happens in your business, but knowing why you're struggling gives you the chance to turn it around.

Client Follow Up

Following up with previous and potential clients is essential to successful freelancing. What do I mean? Once you've worked for a client, let the client know you'd be delighted to work with him/her/them again (only if that's true, of course). Follow up occasionally with emails or even snail mail cards/notes. For potential clients, you need to reach out occasionally to remind them that you exist. If you don't have a process for this, opportunities will fall through the cracks.

How Opportunities Are Lost

Suppose Marianne, a copy editor, gets a call from a potential client who requests a quote on a project. On Monday, Marianne sends the quote, creating a "potential client" folder with information about the potential client (contact information, who referred the client, what was requested, what was sent, etc.) The potential client folder can be an email folder, a Word folder, or even a literal paper folder. It can also be a web application, like Basecamp, or an Excel spreadsheet.

She then starts to work on another project. The potential client never responds to the quote. Marianne, like many freelancers, never follows up after that.

But maybe the email was eaten by a computer glitch and the client assumes Marianne never sent the quote.

Maybe the potential client got the quote, read it, thought Marianne could help the company but, like Marianne, got caught up with his next project and forgot about it.

Maybe the original requester left the company but the new editorial director would like to see the quote. If Marianne has no method of follow-up, a fixable problem is the same thing as a no. Not doing follow up means losing out on many potentially lucrative relationships.

The 5 Steps of Follow-Up

Here are some simple steps to take to make sure follow-up (and follow-through!) happens:

Step 1. Create a System

Come up with a series of steps to take with every potential client. A simple checklist will do the trick. If your checklist has "send follow-ups at one week, one month, and two months after the quote is presented" then as soon as you send the quote, you check the checklist, see that you need to schedule follow-ups, and put them on the calendar.

To keep things simple, I always schedule just one follow-up at a time. Doing that follow-up triggers me to schedule the next one. The schedule says everything I need to know: "October 10: Acme Publishers follow-up #1/schedule #2 for Nov 10."

If Acme responds, then I only have one follow-up to delete from my schedule instead of a handful. If you use Outlook or most online calendars, you can set these as "recurring" and then delete the entire series at any point.

Step 2. Ask the Client

Ask the (potential) client how they prefer the follow-up to occur. Almost all of my work takes place through email and the same is true of most editors. But there are clients who prefer a quick phone call or an instant message. Or even a DM on Facebook or Twitter.

Do what they want (unless you're not on Facebook or Twitter; then find a compromise).

Usually I'll state this as, "I'll email you next month to see where you are in the decision-making process — let me know if you'd prefer a call or another method of follow-up."

If you're in the early stages of client cultivation, the prospective client may not tell you what they want. In that case, go to Step 3.

Step 3. Adapt

If the potential client responds to your email with a phone call or an IM, try using that method yourself. Speak the client's language.

Step 4. Follow-up Without Selling

Follow-up with non-salesy information. Send a link to an article you think a client might be interested in. Provide a white-paper or thought-leadership piece you've written. Don't keep repeating, "Hire me! Hire me!"

Step 5. Stay Patient and Positive

Converting a client can take a while. Stay patient and positive — but don't give up! It's likely to take several contacts to make any progress. Many freelancers give up right after the initial contact. Most give up after the first follow-up. But those who follow-up three or four times often land the client.

Project Management

If you only have one or two clients and one or two projects, it's pretty easy to keep track of what you need to do when. But once you start getting a lot of clients at a lot of different points in the client acquisition process along with a lot of projects at a lot of different stages of completion, it's easy to drop one or more of the balls you're juggling. And that leads to unhappy clients.

I organize client information in folders in Outlook since most of my contact with clients is by email. Under a main folder with the client name, I add subfolders for different projects. If a client sends information about two different projects, I copy the email so one copy goes in each folder. For any email that requires action, I put the task on the to-do list before filing the email.

For longer-term projects and longer-term clients, I also keep a Word document outlining what we've discussed (because often we'll work out details by phone rather than through email). The most recent action goes at the top of the document so that there is a reverse chronological order going on.

You can use client management software, spreadsheets, apps, or even just paper file folders hanging near your desk. If you prefer to use a web application for project management, check out Basecamp, Trello, 17Hats, and Asana.

Start out as simply as possible and then only build in complexity as needed.

What about a project with more moving parts? For example, what if you need to get feedback from the client on Part A before you can begin on Part B? Or you have to incorporate feedback from several stakeholders into one round of edits?

For essential pieces in a project, you need to develop a method for making certain that one action triggers the next. For instance, when you get approval for a quote on a project, that should trigger a few next steps — blocking out time in your schedule to do the work, calling the client to set up a launch meeting, etc.

Project Checklists

At first, you may need to list every single step on a project checklist but over time you'll probably develop a more shorthand routine so that one action logically triggers another without your having to consult a checklist. However, I'm a huge fan of checklists and encourage you to use them even after you've been in business for twenty years. (I do!)

The project checklist should describe the steps you need to do, in chronological order, for the project. Begin your checklist at the very beginning. When someone inquires about your services, what is the first thing you need to do? (You will of course have marketing to-do items before this but that's a separate issue). You will probably need to clarify what the potential client is looking for, determine whether this is a service you offer, decide if it's a good match (you edit mystery and romance but the potential client has a horror novel), take a peek at a sample to make sure the client's idea of what is needed and your idea match up, etc.

The list gets long fast, as you can see — which is why it's so important to have it.

All the components of the project should be listed, from client intake to delivery of the final edit. Forgetting that you've promised to do a round of review until an author email pops up while you're on your long-awaited anniversary trip to Paris is a problem you don't have to have.

Often, contracts will specify elements that must be present, such as when the author will have his/her revision done for your final review (if that is a service you offer). Note these parameters and limitations on the project checklist as well.

As parts of the project come due, note them on your to-do list. (Project management applications can integrate these moving parts so that you don't have to do them manually.)

Projects in Progress

Some freelancers create a master "projects in progress" plan, which can be done using most project management apps or can be managed with a whiteboard hanging on your wall (spreadsheet programs and spiral notebooks also work).

The "projects in progress" plan includes information about all the different projects you have going on. For each project, you list the project name ("Meghan Markle's ms PRINCESS JOURNALS"), the status of the project ("quote sent") and the follow-up that is necessary ("On 10-24, check if Meghan has questions about quote").

Modify this however you want, even keeping track of the hours you work on each project, depending on your needs. At least once a week, simply check the master plan to see what needs to be followed up and to make sure anything that needs to be done is noted on your daily to-do list. If you use a master plan such as this, you need to note status changes in your projects as they occur.

If you're doing this manually, as soon as you send the follow-up email, not only do you have to mark this off your to-do list, you have to mark it off the individual project list, then update the master plan to reflect the next step in the process. Apps will automate these steps.

You can adapt any of these possibilities to better suit your own needs. Or, create your own follow-up system. Sit down and brainstorm something completely unique. Unless you have a detail-oriented, organized mind, you should keep it as simple as possible. The less duplication of effort that follow-up involves, the better.

Chapter 4

Career and Life Management

You'll notice I didn't call this chapter "Work-Life Balance" because hahahahahahahaha!

The best I can promise is management.

The reason freelancers work too much isn't because they love it so much (although that may be true for some people some of the time), it's because it's too easy to work—your laptop's right there—and there's always something you could be doing. Work can quickly take over your personal life. Add in the fact that you might take on too much work because you don't want to decline a project this week only to have no work next week, and you can easily find your quality of life suffering—even if you became a freelancer in order to improve it!

Managing the Work

If you're the one doing all of the work while the cat grooms himself, sometimes your to-do list becomes your mortal enemy. You spend the entire morning responding to emails and sending quotes only to spend the entire afternoon searching for the notes on a phone conversation you had last month. And you still have a stack of your real work waiting for your attention.

Establish Good Habits Early

What to do? Organize your routine so that everything runs as smoothly as possible. And develop good office management skills so that you don't waste time on mundane, unimportant tasks. It's estimated that most business people spend six or more hours a week just trying to find things. That's almost an entire work day. Just think what you could do with an entire day!

When I say "organize" and "routine" a lot of people flinch. They want to freelance to get away from punching a time clock and following rigid schedules. But establishing good habits early on gives you more flexibility and freedom down the road. If you get your work done in an eight-hour day (instead of spending four hours on Candy Crush before you fire up your email inbox), you'll have more free time to pursue a hobby, go for a walk, or play fetch with the dog.

The key to establishing good habits is to work on the most important (not necessarily the most urgent or the easiest) task that will move you toward your goals. This means you need to find a way to sort the important from the unimportant and to get your work done when it needs to be done. Wasting your time—which is valuable—is worse than wasting money because you can always get more money.

This doesn't mean you can never pen a lengthy letter to a dear friend rather than send a quick email, just that you should decide what's important. You should be in control.

The Three-Bucket Approach

Think of your work life as having three buckets, all of which contribute to your success:

- The first bucket should be for the work that makes money (such as editing a client manuscript).
- The second bucket should be for the work that directly supports the work that makes money, such as writing and sending invoices and marketing your services. This might be called the administrative bucket.
- The third bucket should be for the work that is none of the above but which still relates to business goals, such as reading a business book or attending a conference or a class.

If it doesn't belong in one of these buckets, it's not something you should be doing during work hours.

Work on Tasks from All Buckets

The work that makes money (Bucket #1) should be prioritized by due date or project length (longer projects need more room on the schedule) or some combination thereof.

The work that supports the work that makes money (Bucket #2) should be prioritized by the amount of money and the nearness to money that it involves. An invoice for a thousand dollars should come before filing a fifty-dollar claim in the bankruptcy case of a former client.

The work that is none of the above (Bucket #3) should be organized in order of importance to you and your business goals.

Each day, you'll create your to-do list with some combination of items from the various buckets. You should change your thought-out and decided-upon list only when absolutely necessary—not just because someone called and asked you to.

Keep Your Priorities Straight

Remember, someone else's urgency doesn't have to be yours. Your bottom-line question should always be your bottom line: How much is it worth? This is a difficult question for many freelancers to ask, but you need to ask it to keep control of your time.

If an author who plans to pay you fifty dollars for a query letter critique wants it this afternoon, which was when you planned to finish the fee quote for a longtime client that could result in a five-thousand-dollar sale, tell the query author you're sorry about the delay, the best you can do is tomorrow. She will probably accept that. If not, you may have lost a fifty-dollar sale. But it's not worth it to make the fifty dollar sale and lose the five-thousand-dollar sale.

The value of your time and the relative importance of the different demands on your time should guide your thinking as you respond to clients and requests.

As I mentioned above, each day, items from each bucket go on your to-do list, generally in proportion to where you are in your career. Early on you will have less work that brings in income, so you will spend more time on Buckets #2 and #3. As business heats up, you'll spend more time on Buckets #1 and #2. You'll notice that #2 is always important even if you have a lot in #1 to get done.

Time Blocking

It's not enough to just insert items on your to-do list. You need to actually plan the time it takes to do them. This helps ensure you're realistic about what you can accomplish in any given day, helps you keep from over- (or under-) scheduling yourself, and serves to help you stay focused. If it's nine a.m. on Wednesday and the nine a.m. to-do item for Wednesday is to finish the project quote for that indie author, then that's what you're doing.

Everything on your to-do list should have its time blocked out on your calendar. So, if you anticipate an edit will take you eighty hours to complete over the next month, what are the actual days and times you will do the edit? Keep in mind that you're not going to do good work if your answer is five sixteen-hour days.

Don't forget that you need to include items from all three buckets. If your workload is such that you're working sixty-hour weeks just doing the editing (Bucket #1), you need to make a change.

Goals, Goals, Goals

How you figure out your Bucket tasks is by first identifying your important long- and short-term goals. You can be as farfetched as you wish when you're brainstorming, but when it comes time to putting action items on your to-do list, you need to decide which of these goals is worth trying to reach.

Select one or two of the most important long-term goals ("build a thriving editorial business that bills forty thousand dollars in its first year") and commit to it/them.

Then break those long-term goals down into short-term goals. "Build a thriving editorial business" will have several short-term goals associated with it, such as "find three new clients this month" and "create a responsive website where people can find more information about my business."

Once you have a series of building-block goals in place, you can create specific action steps for your to-do list: "Ask colleagues for recommendations re: website designers" and "write a press release to send to the local paper announcing my new business."

Remember how we talked about strategies, tactics, and to-do items in the marketing chapter (Chapter 2)? The same idea applies here. The big goal can't be achieved just by writing it down. You have to determine the actions you need to take to reach it.

Keep in mind that cohesive sets of goals are easier to meet. "Make $80,000 this year" and "work only about ten hours a week" are somewhat contradictory.

Review your long-term goals at intervals, perhaps every quarter. Are you making sufficient progress toward them? You should look at your short-term goals more often, such as once a month. Are you getting closer to meeting them? Are they still important to you? Have new goals come up? By analyzing your goals on a regular basis, you'll keep them in mind and mold your action steps to achieve them.

The Paying Work (Bucket #1)

The paying work is pretty easy to define: you're editing something for someone, right? And you know how to do it, yes? You have a deadline, you've got your butt in chair, go!

The biggest challenge people have with getting things in this bucket done is underestimating how much time it will take. Most of the editors I work with underestimate by as much as thirty-five percent. That's a lot of late nights and weekends. Make sure you're being realistic about what you can actually get done in a given day, week, month.

Time tracking is essential so be sure you're keeping track of how long various tasks take. See the "Time Diary" section below for more on this.

Later in this chapter, I'll talk about keeping your head in the game and staying focused when you'd rather be playing with your cat than trying to figure out just what is wrong with the doorstopper of a manuscript you're looking at now.

Administrative Tasks (Bucket #2)

Administrative tasks, especially if we include fuzzy notions like "marketing" in this category, can swallow up every available moment. Or, alternatively, you can keep putting it off until you default on your mortgage because you haven't sent any invoices for the last six months.

In the very beginning, when you have few clients and even fewer projects, most of your work consists of trying to find work. After that you should be certain to guard the hours in which you produce the paying work as your most precious asset — because it is. (More on guarding productive work time in a bit.)

That means the Bucket #2 items, while important, have to be kept in their proper proportion. You can't spend six hours a day making up cute infographics for Facebook and think that will somehow pay off down the road for you. It won't, unless you want to get hired to make cute infographics for Facebook.

I set aside a certain amount of time each week for administrative tasks — at least five hours but not more than fifteen. This includes catching up my recordkeeping, responding to general inquiry emails, sending out invoices, and marketing my services. I make phone calls, order supplies, and run errands.

I used to do all of this on Tuesday morning. If some of the work overlapped into Tuesday afternoon, that was okay. But once Tuesday was over, I did not do any more administrative tasks, even if I still had some left over (I did the most important work first, so what was left over was usually not that important). I just ignored everything else until the following Tuesday.

This worked for many years until it didn't, which you'll find to be true of many aspects of running your freelance business. I started doing shorter-term work and work that required faster response times. So, I started setting aside an hour each day (usually at lunch, when my attention is flagging anyway). But I only do it during that hour. Then I go back to the paying work.

Once or twice a month I will focus on marketing-related items and this will take up more time. Ordinarily I do these tasks early in the morning or after my regular work hours end. My best times for doing deep work (the actual editing, Bucket #1 work) is from about eight to noon and then from about two to four. So, I schedule Bucket #2 items around those hours.

Everything Else (Bucket #3)

Most of this book deals with how to accomplish the work you'll find in Buckets #1 and #2 because those are the more complex issues. Bucket #3 work is simpler. I mean, if you need to read a book on business principles, well, you know how to read a book, and you don't need me standing on the sidelines explaining how to power on your Kindle.

But I do want to say something about investing in yourself and in your business, because that's what most of the Bucket #3 items are. They're things like taking a class, or going to a conference, or hiring a coach/mentor to help you become more successful.

The challenge here is two-fold. First, there is the temptation to just take classes and go to conferences for the rest of your life without actually doing anything — editing a book or starting a business.

Second (and sort of opposite), there is the temptation to avoid spending much money on these types of professional development opportunities. You don't *need* to go to a conference to succeed. You don't *need* to hire a coach to succeed.

But sometimes going to the conference or hiring the coach can make such a profound impact on your work that it's like getting a year or two additional experience for a few thousand dollars—something that's probably worth every penny. I've gone to conferences where I've met colleagues who've referred work to me worth tens of thousands of dollars. One such colleague—met at a small local conference, of all things—referred me to a job that in five years was worth over a hundred thousand dollars.

I've always felt investment in my professional development should be a line item in my budget, and it is—not just my financial budget but my time budget. It should be a line item on yours, too.

Deciding What's Important

As important as your work is, it's not and shouldn't be the only thing in your life. You need to be sure your work and life goals reinforce each other. Just as "Make a lot of money" and "don't work much" are kind of hard to achieve at the same time, "Build a monolithic editorial empire that bills forty grand a month" and "attend all of Jimmy's soccer games" can be hard to achieve at the same time.

Make a List, Check It Twice

One of the best ways to examine your priorities and to be intentional about them is to make a list of everything important in your life, such as your friends, your family, your work, your pets, your church, your community, and your softball games. Put everything on the list. Then rank the importance of the things that have shown up on your list.

Your Top Three To-Dos

The top three items are what you should spend your time on—and I mean making sure these are the things that you schedule on a daily basis. They are your life priorities and should be treated as such. When you have spare time, attend to other things.

This is not to say that you don't need to meet the duties and obligations that being a civilized person requires of you, such as voting on Election Day and helping little old ladies cross the street. It simply means that you set your priorities and then you stick with them.

After hearing about a famous writer who made such a list, I wrote down everything from the daughter I love to the theatre shows I like to attend. I decided that the most important things in my life were my daughter, my creative work, and my editing career. Everything else, including friends and theatre-going, was less important.

Prioritize, Prioritize, Prioritize

Even within the three top-ranked priorities I made a mental list of importance. For example, I'm always at the hospital with Jessica, but I'll let someone else take her to a routine medical exam. In my creative work, I do what stretches me, intrigues me, excites me whether or not there is likely to be success/money/reward at the end of it. In my editing career, keeping long-term clients happy is more important than trying to sign new clients.

Identifying my priorities allows me to constantly re-dedicate myself to what is truly important to me instead of getting sidetracked by other people's priorities.

When I can fit in coffee with old friends, I do so. But when the choice is between my daughter and my former office mate, my daughter takes precedence.

Write out your top three priorities and put them where you'll see them every day. Then ask yourself if what you're doing right now is related to any of the top three priorities. If not, quit doing it.

Ask the Right Questions

Before accepting any request for your time and involvement in any activity, ask yourself if it furthers one of your top three priorities.

If your child's school asks you to be the teacher's assistant one afternoon a week, think about your priorities before you decide. Would it mean a lot to your child if you did?

Don't worry about what the teacher will think or what the school administrator will say or what opinion the neighbors will have. None of them are on your priority list. Your child is. If it matters to your child and how much it matters (plus how much time you have to spare) should be your only considerations.

As a freelancer, you don't have a boss telling you what to do anymore. It's surprisingly easy to get sucked into doing what other people want you to do, even if it negatively affects your work and personal life.

Daily Planning

In order to keep on top of your projects and your business, you'll need two things: a to-do list and a calendar. You can use a paper planner if you like going old school, but Outlook also works, as does your phone's calendar/scheduling function. Use whatever makes sense for you, what you're already using, or what you'll be most likely to use. Reconsider using anything that creates any kind of barrier. If your phone is always in the other room when it's time to use its scheduling function, try something else.

The calendar is for noting down appointments, which require you to be at a certain place at a certain time on a certain day. Relying on your memory to warn you of an upcoming appointment is foolhardy at best. A to-do list is to note down everything else you need to do.

Basics of Task Scheduling

As I mentioned above, I combine both using time blocking. I schedule specific times on my calendar for doing specific to-do list tasks. If a task is triggered (for example, a quote is agreed to), I immediately schedule the next action item on my calendar. If something doesn't get done (I underestimated how much time a project would take, I came down with the flu and couldn't finish a task), I re-schedule it immediately. This helps ensure that tasks get done and keeps me aware of how the work flow is going. If I'm constantly rescheduling to-do items, something's wrong.

This approach works for me because I have a lot of control over my schedule and generally don't have more than five or six to-do items on any given day.

Whatever you do, don't use a bunch of different calendars that need to be reconciled. Keep personal and business items on the same calendar to avoid confusion.

If you need a public-facing calendar so that clients can pop themselves in, then be sure it integrates smoothly with your main calendar. If you have to manually transfer information from one to the other, something is likely to be overlooked.

The To-Do List

Your to-do list guides your work in a given day. It should contain the most important items from your three buckets (work, admin, miscellaneous-related-to-business). If you're not using time blocking, then items should be organized according to importance to ensure that the most important things get done first.

Some people make to-do lists that rival the invasion of Normandy for complexity and ambition. They have long-term goals and short-term goals and business goals and personal goals and monthly goals and yearly goals and then somehow get frustrated when nothing gets done.

To-Do List Items Are Tasks

A goal is not a to-do item. A goal is a goal. You may want to make fifty grand this year. That would be a goal. Sending out five letters of introduction every day in order to reach that goal is a to-do item. You may want to become the most sought-after developmental editor in the US. Becoming a sought-after editor is a goal, not a to-do item. Doing the editing that will help you achieve that status is a to-do item.

As more to-do activities are generated, either because someone has created one (asking for a quote on a project, for example) or because you thought of one ("I should let my former boss know I'm freelancing now. He might be able to use the help.") add them to your schedule or put them on the to-do list next to tasks of similar importance.

Make Accurate Time Estimates

Editors constantly underestimate how long it takes to do a thorough edit, and then wonder why they never seem able to get on top of their work load. In truth, editors aren't the only ones who do this — there's a name for it (Optimist's Fallacy) but you don't have to be an optimist to suffer from it.

Keeping track of how long various items take will help you develop, over time, a clearer sense of what is realistic for you to accomplish in a given day.

Group Similar Tasks

If you have a lot of one type of task, such as phone calls to make or quick emails to write, you might just group them together instead of trying to determine order of importance. The only caution is not to spend too much time on low-priority tasks. If an unimportant email starts taking up more than five minutes of your time, abandon it and move on.

I don't keep separate to-do lists for personal and business activities, although I know some freelancers do. I just keep my personal activities listed in a "personal stuff" section of the list. Then, when I'm making phone calls for business reasons, I can slip that personal phone call in there too, as long as it doesn't take up too much time, and as long as it's something I need to do during business hours.

Emails and Phone Calls

Handling email seems to be the most difficult task freelancers have. Often people are advised to respond to an email when it is received so that it doesn't stay and clutter up the inbox. That's certainly efficient but it's not rational. Your goal isn't to have inbox zero because it's so pretty. Your goal is to get your work done, not to act on every single stimulus that comes your way.

The key to taking control of business is to act, not react. If I let the pile of email I get every half hour dictate what I'm doing, then I'm reacting, not acting. I'm not determining what's important; I'm letting the whim of the people emailing me do it. This is not the way to run a business.

Use a Disciplined Approach

Instead, check email only a few times a day. Use folders to sort incoming email so that important items don't get overlooked, note down any work that needs to be done on your to-do list/calendar, and delete the rest.

Use folders and subfolders so everything doesn't sit in your inbox in a huge undigested lump, forcing you to scan through three hundred vague and repetitive subject lines to find what you want. Archive project information when the project is complete and the invoice paid.

More Can Be Better

Consider using a throwaway email address (like Gmail or Yahoo — where you don't have to pay for the service) for uses that won't require your urgent attention, such as to sign up for a newsletter. You can check the throwaway account occasionally and keep these low-importance items out of your main inbox.

You might also think about having a public-facing email address ("info@" or something similar) that you use for general inquiries. This is the email address you would use on your website and anywhere your contact information will appear online. Only use your main address for current clients. You can set up an autoresponder for "info@" inquiries so that potential clients know you've received their email but you don't have to respond immediately. This will also help reduce the amount of spam your main email address gets.

If this sounds like a recipe for spending three times as much time on email as you do now, then feel free to disregard. Different approaches work for different people.

Phone Calls

In order to handle phone conversations effectively, you need to have immediate access to any information the client might refer to. For this reason, client files are indispensable, as I mentioned in Chapter 3. I keep a folder in my email management system for every client and put all correspondence there.

But it can be difficult to dig through all the emails we've sent back and forth to find the one fact I need during a phone call, so I also keep an editorial checklist for each client that covers what we've agreed to and what the edit will contain. There are other ways to manage this—just pick what works for you and stick with it.

Keep Records

Make a record of every phone conversation you have and put the notes in the appropriate client file, first noting any to-do actions on your list. Make sure you include the date of the conversation. This will help you document what was discussed. For clients, I summarize what was discussed and email it to them, copying myself. (I am often told this feels like a tremendous added value but it's merely intended to keep me organized.)

Schedule Most Calls

I make it clear that client conversations need to be scheduled. I don't answer unscheduled calls. You may not be so rigid but you can encourage calls at certain times of day when they won't be so disruptive ("I'm more available in the mornings").

Be prepared for phone calls with a list of what you need to cover during the call and what you want to say. Not all dev editors use client phone calls as part of their editorial process, but all of us will occasionally need to clear up a misunderstanding or help an author brainstorm from time to time.

The key is to control as much as possible: make the time and place work for you and keep the conversation focused so that you don't spend a lot of time unproductively.

Establishing Your Freelance Practice

You may say that getting established as a freelancer is a priority, but saying is not doing. You have to develop a practice or a habit of doing the work — marketing, networking, editing. Picking the same time and place every day, or at least on regular days throughout the week, helps you associate that time and place with doing the work.

This can be a challenge if you have a day job, and/or children, and/or other obligations. You can get from morning shower to bedtime story without fifteen minutes to spare. Just because you want to freelance doesn't mean the time is going to magically appear.

I liken it to saving money. If you think you'll save whatever's left of your paycheck after you've paid the bills and bought the groceries and maybe splurged on a movie, you probably won't save anything.

Time is the same way. If you think you'll find the time to freelance after you do everything else, it's likely that you won't. So, just as the way to build your savings is to take 10 percent off the top of your paycheck and live on the rest, you have to book the time first, even if that means eliminating other things you like to do.

Keep a work schedule and stick to it. If you don't have a schedule, you'll either work all day and half the night, and that's no way to run a life, or you'll work when you feel like it, and that's no way to run a business.

While it's true that small business owners work longer hours than employees, some of that time is wasted and could be put to better use. Sometimes freelancers get into a habit of procrastination—"Well, if I wanted I could start work at ten and keep working until seven."

Make Decisions Once

Research shows that the more decisions we force ourselves to make in a given day, the sooner we start making poor decisions. If you keep having to make a decision about when to start work, by the time you're at you're desk, you've already used up a lot of your decision-making power.

If you then start in on a game of, "What task should I start with?" you'll never finish.

Developing a work schedule and creating good habits (e.g., sticking with the work schedule!) will make it easier for you to accomplish your work and have time for the other things you want to do.

It's *Your* Schedule

You don't have to work eight-to-five or nine-to-five or any of the standard business hours. Flexibility is one of the benefits of freelancing. Some of your business hours should be held during the typical business day so that you can reach others and they can reach you. But who's to say you can't work from three in the afternoon to midnight if that suits your rhythms? One of the reasons you're in business for yourself is so you can do as you prefer.

If you can't live without a certain daytime television show, by all means make a spot for it in your schedule. But put structure in your day or you'll drive yourself nuts and you won't get anything done.

By this same reasoning, I suggest if you're going to play hooky, you do it with your whole heart instead of dithering over it. "Oh, it's a beautiful day to go for a walk! But I must get work done. But we don't get many days like this in the middle of winter! But I must get work done." No. Make the decision, take the day off and enjoy every splendid minute of it.

Taking Your Work Seriously

Maintaining a set work schedule is part of taking your own work seriously. In my first year or two of freelancing, I had trouble setting boundaries. When friends called up to chat, I would answer the phone — then complain that they never seemed to understand that I was working. People constantly asked me for favors without doing anything in return. They assumed I could babysit or run errands or do whatever they needed because they were at work and I wasn't.

Then I realized that I needed to act like I was an employee. If I'd been in my office at the university, none of my friends would have called up just to chat or expected me to watch their kids "for just a minute." I decided to start treating my home office the same way.

It doesn't matter if your jealous neighbors think you sit around eating bon-bons all day as long as *you* take your work seriously. That means setting boundaries, getting work done on time, and devoting attention to the less interesting parts of building your business, such as marketing.

Optimize Your Physical Space

If every time you need to work you have to go to the basement to dig out the folding table you rest your laptop on, you're adding a barrier, and barriers keep us from doing things. This is fine if you're trying to restrain yourself from eating all the chocolate, and not so useful if you're trying to establish a freelancing business.

Organization of your physical space allows for efficiency, productivity, and even creativity. Yes, creativity! Editing, especially dev editing, is a creative art. It's also a process that takes a lot of time and space, which you won't have if you're constantly trying to find your red pen.

Even though most of your work will be done on computer and even if you use *The Chicago Manual of Style* website instead of the four-pound tome itself, you will likely need a space to jot down notes and keep your mug of tea, a picture of your adoring family, and any frequently used supplies.

You should have a dedicated work area, not a corner of the kitchen table you have to clear off every afternoon in order to make dinner. It doesn't necessarily have to be a home office with a door that closes. But it does have to be a place where you can keep your stuff and not have to move it every fifteen minutes.

Part of taking your work seriously means finding a way to carve out a corner of space for yourself. For a long time, mine was a walk-in closet in my daughter's bedroom. I stuck a folding table and a good chair in there and went to work. Now I have a dedicated office, but the closet worked fine.

You may have to rearrange as your needs change and as your business evolves, but you should begin with an arrangement that suits what your imagination tells you you'll need and then make adjustments as reality plays its role.

At the end of the day, clean up your work space so that you can find what you need for the next morning, but don't put away everything that you'll just have to get back out again. If you're in the middle of a complicated project, there's nothing wrong with leaving notes and reference books spread out on your desk so that you can pick up where you left off. Just take care of the essentials, like washing out your coffee cup before a mold colony grows in it.

I always review my next day's schedule and to-do list and make any necessary adjustments before turning off the computer for the evening.

Develop Focus

You've set your priorities, decided establishing your freelance editing business is one of them, made some room in your schedule, and now you're sitting at your desk at the same time every day. Still, somehow, the marketing/editing/whatever isn't getting done.

There's nothing wrong with you. You just have to develop focus. Focus isn't something you're magically born with, it's something you learn how to do.

Begin with an hour. Try to work continuously for that hour, without stopping to message a friend, or check Facebook, or answer emails. Just work on your task for an hour, nonstop. It's hard to do.

But don't beat yourself up. Every time your attention wanders, just bring it back to the task at hand. It's like meditation. Notice that you've lost focus, then bring it back to your work.

Some freelancers like to use rituals to segue into and out of their work time. I used to do yoga exercises to signal that I was focusing on my work and then to signal that I was moving to something else, like picking up my daughter from school.

If you let email and texts and the urge to check out cat videos on Facebook interrupt doing the work, you'll struggle. The work won't get done on time, or doing it will require you to use up time that should have been spent on your personal life and relationships. Plus, developing the bad habit of superficial attention will literally make the work harder to do. Most of the work you'll do (developmental editing, copyediting, coaching) requires significant focus and concentration. Sticking with it requires practice.

Banish Interruptions

Other than scheduled breaks, try not to allow interruptions. Set clear rules for others so they know what to expect. Use signals like leaving your office door ajar when interruptions are okay and shutting it when interruptions are not okay. If you need, hire a babysitter to attend to children while you're working, even if you think your children are old enough to fend for themselves.

A number of my colleagues tell me their spouses are the worst offenders. You can't hire a babysitter for your spouse but you can set your boundaries firmly from the beginning (or, do things that break up bad habits, like go to work at the coffee shop for a couple of afternoons a week).

You also have to prevent you from interrupting yourself. Set specific times for different tasks. The idea isn't that you can never play on Facebook. The idea is that you have to be intentional about what you're doing. If it's "play on Facebook" time, then have at it.

Note: One of the problems that creates lack of focus is lack of clarity. If you don't know what you should or could be doing, or you could be doing a hundred things, it's hard to focus. Remember to figure out your goals and work out a series of action steps to reach them. Those action steps will be what you work on during your focused work time.

Schedule Real Breaks

Effective editors tend to do their best work in two- and three-hour blocks of time. After each block, they take a break to clear their minds, then work for another two- or three-hour block of time. Ideally, the break between shouldn't be more than ten or fifteen minutes.

Taking breaks after a concentrated work session is an important part of productivity. But often as freelancers we try to fill up the break time by doing something useful. If you've put in two or three hours of solid work on an edit, switching tasks to something like answering emails or updating your records can feel like a welcome change.

But it's easy to get bogged down in counter-productive actions, such as thinking, "I have to finish recording all these receipts before I go back to my main project." There's no reason why all of your receipts have to be recorded this minute. Some of them can wait until tomorrow morning or next Tuesday.

This is hard for the Type A people who are often attracted to owning their own businesses, but it's okay to leave some tasks undone and finish them at a later time. Don't let the "this task isn't finished" thought trigger the "therefore I need to work on this task" action.

Instead, ask: "Is this what I should be doing right now?" Use your carefully thought-out to-do list to help you answer this question.

Some people use timers to signal when the break is up, which works if you're the kind of person who doesn't keep hitting the snooze button on the alarm in the morning.

Another option is to have small five- and ten-minute tasks to do ("Call the dentist for cleaning") during these brief breaks, but remember to only do one task before going back to the main project for the day.

If you focus on completing two- and three-hour work sessions and use brief breaks for routine tasks, you'll finish your work with time to spare while still sending out invoices on a regular basis. You'll be setting priorities and attending to the important work first instead of getting mired in trivia.

Yes, there will still be the occasional day where everything gets completely out of control and you accomplish nothing, but those days will be fewer and fewer as you organize your efforts.

Keep Calm and Invoice On

In my work, I've discovered that the challenges that prevent freelancers from succeeding fall into four related but in many ways distinct categories:

- habit- and productivity-related (finding the time)
- craft-related (lacking the skill to know what to do next)
- negative-thinking-related (wondering who'd ever want to work with us)
- motivation-related (having no real reason, such as a deadline, to market your services and get clients)

Keep in mind that these challenges can be connected; if you have trouble believing anyone would ever want to hire you (problem #3), you're going to have trouble finding the time to market (problem #1).

Finding Time

The most common complaint freelancers have is that there's never enough time to do everything that needs to be done. But while that may feel true, you *can* find the time to do the work, successfully and lucratively. It comes down to making a choice—it's a simple decision but it's one you have to keep making over and over.

Many choices can free up time. You can choose to devote some evening or weekend hours to your work. Or you can rearrange your schedule to take better advantage of high-energy times. Do productive work when you're most focused and alert, which is probably an hour or so after you wake. Use time when you're less focused for chores that require less attention, like doing the dishes or setting appointments. Don't waste good, productive time on tasks that don't require your full attention and awareness.

Get your family, if you have one, invested in your success. Ask them to help you find the time and keep your schedule clear. They can also be persuaded to make fewer demands on your time. (You may have to insist at first).

Give Up Some Things

Eliminate the "shoulds" that you're doing but don't find particularly rewarding. For example, you should have a vegetable garden, or you should vacuum every day, or you should whatever it might be. If you gave up one of those shoulds, you'd have more time for freelancing. It's okay to be selfish or feel selfish. Really.

I love television as much as the next person, which is why I gave away my television eighteen years ago and have never purchased another one. It's not that I think television is bad, or that it rots your brain — on the contrary, you can learn a lot about stories from some of the shows on television. It's just that I know I'll sit in front of it twenty hours a day if it's available. Your unproductive thing may be Candy Crush or Twitter or OkCupid. Delete, delete, delete.

Schedule the Time

You're not going to miraculously find the time to freelance. You have to schedule it. Years ago a friend of mine told me the secret to her success: she took the first two hours of the day for herself, and then the rest was for everyone else. I started following her example and use those two hours for my creative work. I don't schedule anything else then, not meetings for my regular work, not doctor's appointments, not anything. I just say, "I'm booked in the mornings till 10 a.m., can we do it at 10:30?" and don't have a problem. You can use the same approach for starting your editing business.

Now, this works best if you have a lot of control over your schedule. If you don't, you may have to be creative, like scheduling the work during your bus commute, or on your lunch break, or maybe you get up an hour earlier, or maybe you stay an hour later at the office. Maybe you hire a mother's helper a few times a week, or swap childcare with the neighbor across the street.

A colleague has lately been speaking in praise of fifteen minute blocks of time. As long as he gets a couple of these a day, he can be very productive. Don't rule out opportunities just because they're not dressed up as two-hour blocks of time with no other commitments.

But in any case remember to *schedule* the time to do the work instead of thinking that you'll somehow find it.

Time Diary

One of the most important things you can do, especially as you begin your freelance career, is to keep track of how you spend your time. This seems like a cumbersome chore at first, and it is, but it's extremely effective in (a) showing you how much time it actually takes to do the work and (b) showing you how much time you waste on Facebook.

Most editors underestimate both (and by Facebook I mean any unproductive activity — going down the rabbit hole of "I just need to check this fact" and coming up forty minutes later with newfound knowledge of the symptoms of ptomaine poisoning and which dog breed won Westminster this year but no better understanding of how to spell commitment.)

The time diary doesn't have to be complicated — every half hour or so just note down what you did the previous half hour. Toggl is a popular app for tracking time; there are others. You don't have to use an app — you can use a scrap piece of paper or a Word document. The challenge isn't in the method, it's in having the discipline to make the notes, so pick whatever method is easiest.

Whenever you feel pressed for time, try keeping a time diary. This will help you make decisions based on facts, not just impressions. For example, I always think my monthly newsletter takes an hour or two to write and send. The reality is that it usually takes four or five hours. When I dig deeper, I see most of this time is spent on sourcing images! Who even notices the images in my newsletter? Just because the Mailchimp template has a spot for images doesn't mean I need to plug them in.

Maybe some of your most time-consuming chores can be farmed out or eliminated. Maybe you need to rethink your processes and your ways of doing things. Maybe you need to make more money per project and take on fewer projects. Keeping a time diary will help you make decisions wisely, based on facts rather than on inaccurate guesses.

Mastering the Craft

Craft-related challenges crop up when you don't know how to do what you need to do next, are unsure whether you're going in the right direction, have never encountered a particular editing problem before, or have but aren't convinced you know how to solve it.

Sometimes fear of encountering these challenges stops us from even getting started. Other times, these concerns mean we don't finish a project, even if we've agreed to, or we're reluctant to take on anything that presents a challenge because we're not sure we'll succeed.

Google Is Your Friend

Craft-related challenges are sometimes pretty obvious. We get to a certain part of the ms, think, "I don't quite know the best way to edit the head-hopping in this scene" and set the ms aside. Then maybe we never quite go back to it. Or maybe we glide over the problem scene but our confidence takes a hit and we decide not to take on another project like that (in that genre, from that writer, whatever).

Often the answer is to do some research or outreach, such as reading books and blog posts on the subject; attending classes or a conference; or asking colleagues (joining an editor's group is a great way to find such colleagues).

You have many resources to help you improve your craft. It's just a matter of connecting the dots.

Just Do the Work

Craft-related challenges don't always present themselves so clearly. If they always showed up as, "I don't know how to effectively edit a head-hopping scene," then you'd probably have a fair idea of how to solve them. Often they show up as just a general frustration with the work. You know there's something wrong with the scene in this ms but you can't quite put your finger on it.

The solution to this might seem to be what I mentioned before (read books, ask colleagues) but often the solution is more straightforward: just do the edit — even though you're doing a sucky job at it.

An artist friend of mine has lately been trying to teach me how to draw something other than stick figures, and my progress is incremental (that is to say, it is agonizingly slow). I'd love to be able to do what she does, but I can't. Not right now, anyway. But if all I ever aspire to is stick figures, I'll never improve.

Same with the editing. Maybe stick figures are all you're capable of now, but the aspiration itself is part of what makes you better. If you think stick figures are the bomb and you don't try to do better, you won't do better. But you also won't do better if you think, "I can't draw that gorgeous landscape in front of me right now so I may as well not even try."

My artist friend says, "Your perception always runs ahead of your skill." You always see what you want to be able to do better than you can actually do it.

I don't mean that in a discouraging way; it's actually very helpful to realize that as your perception of what good editing is sharpens, your skills will sharpen, too.

Put it this way: When you're five, you don't know that you're drawing stick figures and that they suck. That one day you recognize that you're drawing stick figures is huge progress in your maturation as an artist (or an editor).

So: write an imperfect edit, realize that it's imperfect, try to do better. Lather, rinse, repeat.

For specific technical issues that may be causing a problem for you, check out the "What Now?" section at the end of this book.

Defeating Negative Nelly

Often freelancers talk about the "no": "Well, that project wasn't meant to be," or "There were so many red flags, I didn't follow up." And that's fine; I get that some editing projects don't go anywhere and some potential clients don't pan out. You're better off spending your time and energy on projects more likely to lead to fruition.

But my general position is that when you're first starting out, you need to say yes a whole lot more than you say no.

If you're anything like me, what you want from your freelancing career is to get a bunch of clients to pay you good money to fund your living expenses, not to mention add a little chunk of change to your retirement account.

But if you're anything like me, this is hard. Potential clients do not automatically convert to paying clients, money does not land in your bank account without massive effort, and projects go south from time to time despite your best efforts to keep them moving.

Cue Negative Nelly.

She's that oh-so-annoying voice in your head that says, "Why are you locked in your office trying to build a freelancing business no one cares about when you could be having sex with that cabana boy?" Maybe the cabana boy is a figment of my imagination but the rest is pretty familiar, right?

My Negative Nelly thinks I could be earning real money, losing weight, being a better mother, saving the world, and telling those kids to stay off my lawn if only I didn't spend so much time trying to get people to pay me to edit their words. Who do I think is going to care that I can help them create a better story? I might as well watch *Tangled* again instead for all the difference it will make.

Also, remember how I've made mistakes before? Negative Nelly doesn't want me to forget. Just in case I was laboring under a delusion of competence. She doesn't know why I bother. When she thinks of all those lost opportunities — do I remember that time I turned down a date so I could work on a project quote that was turned down? I'm going to die friendless and alone and also I will be buried in an unmarked grave because no one will even remember who I am.

Ahem. Nelly has had a long, long time to hone her craft and she's very good. She knows just where to stick the knives.

Banish Nelly

I've lived with Nelly for many years, and for a sorry number of them I listened to her. Finally, I realized that she wasn't helping anything. Even if she was right about my competence, giving up wasn't going to make me a better editor, was it?

I also recognized that the options weren't usually saving the world or working on my business, but they tended to be watching a movie or working on my business, or cleaning the house or working on my business. Every time Nelly started in about saving the world, I pointed out that I could also be a meth addict instead of a freelancer, or a Mafioso instead of a freelancer. The world isn't made up of either/or, but a spectrum of ways we can live. Freelance editing can integrate into almost any of them.

A friend of mine makes Nelly go sit on the porch when she's working. Another sends hers to Tahiti. Both have little rituals they use to banish Nelly before they start writing. Give it a try.

Just the Facts, Ma'am

Sometimes Nelly presents herself as just a big roiling ball of fear. Fear of success, fear of failure, fear of sucking, fear of not knowing you suck, fear of pretty much everything. Instead of letting that big ball of fear stop you, open it up. What, actually, does Nelly think is going to happen if you keep trying?

She'll tell you, if you listen. She'll say, If you take the risk and freelance instead of staying at your day job, maybe you won't make enough to pay the bills. If you keep the day job and try to freelance on the side, maybe you'll get distracted from your day job and wind up fired. If you invest in starting a freelance business, maybe you won't spend enough time with your kids and they'll grow up to be hoodlums. Maybe maybe maybe.

Often, once you know what that big ball of fear is about, you can do something to address it. Maybe you do need to work on your craft. The answer isn't to let Nelly stop you. The answer is to take a class or read a book.

When Nelly starts in with "You'll never get any clients," thank her for her concern, but remind her that a lot of people do establish successful freelance editing businesses. If she says this edit sucks, tell her she may be right but the next one will be better.

Nelly is a nuisance, but letting her stop you is a choice. Don't keep making it.

Let the Good Times Roll

I keep a folder called Nice Things People Say About Me on my computer. Whenever someone compliments me on my work, I put it in the folder. When Negative Nelly gets going, I'll take a peek at the contents of that folder to remind myself that someone who isn't me thinks I do good work.

I also keep an accomplishment list so that I can remind myself of projects that worked out. I list projects I've worked on, awards the books I've edited have been nominated for and/or won, anything like that. When I first started, the accomplishment list was more about marketing tasks, like sending out letters of introduction. It doesn't matter what stage of your career you're at, you're accomplishing something that you can keep on the list.

This helps when I get nineteen "thanks, but no thanks" responses in a single week and Negative Nelly starts up.

Confronting Nelly

Sometimes you can ignore Nelly and she'll go away. But sometimes she doesn't. When she's got you by the throat, it may help to confront the thinking. First, write down what your negative thoughts are. They might be things like, "I'll never get any clients" or "I can never stand out against the competition" or "No one values my skills." Just list them all on a page. Sometimes just getting them out can help you turn your attention back to doing the work.

If that's not enough, take the next step. Look at each negative thought in turn and ask yourself how you know it to be true. If you think, "I'll never get any clients" then challenge that idea. Why won't you get clients? Go to an editors' organization like the Editorial Freelancers Association or Editors' Association of Earth (a Facebook group) and you'll see lots of people are getting clients. You could certainly be one of them.

If Nelly says you're pawning your financial security, look at your bank account. Is it true? Probably not. If Nelly says you're sacrificing your children's future, look at your kids. Is it true? Probably not.

If the answer is yes, then okay, maybe you do have some work to do. But almost certainly Nelly is doing what she does best, fear-mongering.

Next, challenge yourself to think of the negative thought in a new way. When you say, "I'll never get clients," you're probably thinking of a very specific type of thing, like, "I'll never be able to get enough clients to make six figures without putting a tremendous effort into it."

Well, okay, you probably won't. But if it's just a question of one client—surely you can find one client somewhere, even if you have to work for beer money.

Finally, ask yourself, "So what?" Okay, so you don't ever get one single client, ever, under any circumstances, even offering to work for free. You'll still have a good life, won't you? I hope you will. I expect you will. Asking yourself "So what?" keeps this whole endeavor in perspective. You can have a great life, and even be a skilled editor, and not necessarily rock it as a freelancer. But don't let negative thinking stop you from trying. Deal?

Focus on the Process

In the end, mostly our negative thinking comes down to uncertainty. We don't know if we'll ever achieve what we want to achieve. Even if we do finish writing the quote/letter of introduction/insert task here, there's nothing to say anyone will respond to it. And even if we do every possible thing we know how to do to be successful, there are no guarantees. We cannot control the outcome.

That fact is so very annoying.

In the end we have to remember that the process is what matters, and we need to focus on that. In other words, are you doing the work? Focusing on the process puts the emphasis where it belongs, on what you can control.

Finding the Motivation

You know you want to establish a freelance editing business, but somehow you just can't get motivated to apply butt to chair and get it done. It may be that what's stopping you is a productivity-related problem (you don't have time), or you're stuck and don't know what to do next (craft-related troubles), or you're letting negative thinking stop you (we went over all of these earlier in the chapter).

But it could just be that without any deadline and with no rewards in sight, it's hard to give "start freelancing!" any kind of urgency. There's always going to be something else that could use your attention. Even helping out at the PTA bake sale would be more fulfilling. At least someone will say thank you, right?

So how do you motivate yourself without guarantee of reward? Previously, I talked about focusing on the process, and I think that's key. If you enjoy the process, then the outcome matters less.

"But wait!" you say. "I enjoy editing but I hate marketing. I have to market but it's a process I *don't* like — and I'm never going to like it. Now what?"

Commit to Your Work

In Chapter 1, I talked about all the reasons why you're freelancing — your purpose as an editor as well as your personal reasons why this is the right choice for you. Remember that purpose. It can help you stay on task, even if you don't feel like it. Even when you're marketing.

A public statement of purpose can be a very powerful tool to motivate you to make progress. If you tell all your Facebook friends that you're going to send out ten letters of introduction this week, you're more motivated to get it done because you'll feel the need to let them know you succeeded.

I've used this technique to great success when I've had a tough slog. I'll post an update saying I have 5,000 words to edit and I'll start counting down, commenting as I get closer and closer to my goal. It's amazing how many people chime in and urge me on. I don't want to disappoint them, so I get it done.

Making It Formal

Sometimes you need to make a more formal pact regarding your commitment. I've used accountability partners for years and find them extremely helpful for keeping me on task. Basically, the process works by my finding a like-minded freelancer who has some long-term goals.

Each week we figure out what tasks for that week would give us significant progress toward that long-term goal (or goals) and make those tasks a priority.

We send our to-do lists to each other. Then we check in with each other midweek. If one of us is struggling, the other will help brainstorm solutions, offer resources, or just lend an ear. Often that's enough to get unstuck.

Then we end the week with a statement of what we accomplished. Sometimes we'll include something we learned about ourselves, the goal, or the process. Then we say what our tasks for the next week will be. Sometimes these relationships have gone on for years.

I've also done a boot camp version of this with a friend. We devote one day to making a big chunk of progress. We make a plan at the start of the day, then call each other every hour and report in: what we've done this hour and what we're going to do the next. It's amazing how well this approach works.

Be aware that if you start letting each other get away with excuses, the process stops working effectively. Yes, life happens and gets in the way of completing tasks, and there's no point in beating yourself or each other up over that. But you should be able to get back on track afterwards, and to make some amount of progress, no matter how small, even during an otherwise challenging time. Be willing to ask each other the tough questions.

Incentivize

Some people reward themselves for doing the work. If they meet their goals by Friday, they get to take the weekend off. If they finish a marketing task, they get a treat. What that treat is varies from person to person — chocolate, an afternoon in the park, a pedicure, a new pen.

A small reward can give you a visible token of your progress, especially when your work seems otherwise unrewarding. A friend and I used to send each other such tokens whenever we met important goals. So I'd report success in reaching a milestone and I'd get a fun package in the mail. I still remember my delight in receiving a rainbow set of Sharpies (this happened more than ten years ago, and I remember the Sharpies!)

Another way to incentivize is to create a visual map of your progress. Hang a calendar on your wall and for every day you do one marketing task (for example), draw in a big fat happy face. Use a big red X on days you didn't do the task. Pretty soon you'll be focusing on not putting any red Xs on the calendar.

Create Artificial Deadlines

Sometimes working to meet a deadline is all the motivation you need. Look ahead on your calendar. Do you have a significant date that you could tie a deadline to? Suppose your class reunion is coming up and you'd like to be able to talk about your success with your new business. Peg your short-term goal(s) and to-do list to that deadline. A graduation, a retirement, a birthday, a vacation—all of these can serve as markers for doing certain tasks related to building your business.

Deadlines that are more closely tied to your actual business can work even better. A conference or class that includes feedback on some portion of your work can serve as a motivating deadline.

Games People Play

Sometimes your inner "I don't wanna!" won't listen to reason, and when that happens to me, I play some sort of silly game. For example, I set the timer for twenty minutes and see how many words I can edit in that amount of time. Then I'll set it for another twenty minutes to see if I can beat my score. Yeah, I know, but it's more productive than Candy Crush, right?

Speaking of Candy Crush . . . if you're having trouble staying focused, you can use a similar game. Give yourself fifteen minutes in which you won't check out Facebook. Then increase the challenge—make it half an hour. This seems silly but it is literally how you build focus.

I'm skilled at turning anything into a game. I'll challenge myself to fill all the pages in my notebook with marketing ideas, no matter how far-fetched, or give myself just five minutes to research and resolve that stupid computer glitch I'm having.

I'm sure you can find similar challenges that take the focus off how much you hate _____ (fill in the blank).

The less you dwell on negative thoughts, the less influence they have over your actions.

Don't just assume that there's something wrong with you or your work if you can't always find the motivation to do it. Develop some strategies and tactics that will help you stay on course even during those times when you don't particularly feel like it.

Once you've identified what's stopping you and why, the solution is at hand. You can do this! It's just a matter of giving yourself the help you need to get it done.

Chapter 5

The Money Talk

In Chapter 1, I talked about defining what you want from your business in overall terms. Now I'm going to get into the dollar discussion. I'll start this off by saying I'm not a fan of setting financial goals as a new freelancer because you can't control how quickly your efforts will bear fruit. Maybe you'll land three new clients your first month out. Maybe it will take you four months to get your first nibble. I don't know and neither do you.

But what I do want you to do is figure out how much you need to charge clients to make a reasonable living. You would not believe the number of freelancers I hear from in a panic—they've got tons of clients and they're doing tons of work but they're about to get evicted (or have other dire financial problems) because they're not charging enough.

Setting Your Fees

Setting fees appropriately means the difference between running a profitable editing business and one that doesn't break even.

First, you need to know how long it will take to do the edit. To know that, you'll have to reach an understanding with the client regarding what your edit will cover. And you'll need to identify what shape the manuscript is in. A manuscript that has something going badly wrong on every page obviously takes more time and effort to edit than a more accomplished manuscript. Therefore, you should charge less for the easier ms and more for the harder ms.

Note that some editors charge a flat fee for a standard edit. For example, they may charge two cents per word. This is easy for everyone to calculate but it does not take into account the relative difficulty of editing different manuscripts. All it takes into account is actual length, which isn't the best measure of the time and effort required to produce an effective edit. Because it's so easy to undercharge for more difficult manuscripts, I discourage taking this approach.

A general rule of thumb says an experienced editor can do a developmental edit (that is to say, an edit focused on overall developmental feedback but with attention paid to sentence-level concerns) of four-to-six pages of 250 words each in about an hour (or: 1000 to 1500 words per hour).

If your client is just asking for overall feedback, you can probably go faster, but if your client is looking for a heavier edit or you're doing a copyedit and the manuscript needs a lot of work, you're probably going to go at this rate or slower.

Bear in mind that your level of experience, the shape the manuscript is in, and other factors will affect your editing speed. I offer this only as a way to make an extremely general guesstimate of how long a project will take to edit.

It helps to know the prevailing rate for various editing tasks. Sometimes the prevailing rate for a particular service is $25 to $500 an hour, which isn't very helpful. But for other services, the prevailing rate is a bit more standardized. A publishing house may pay $25 an hour for proofreading (and probably won't expect to get it for much less), but won't be willing to pay more than $50 (except for very specialized material).

Try Googling "Editorial services" + "fees" to find fee schedules on the websites of other freelance editors to see what they're charging for services you plan to offer.

Also, you can consult market rate lists developed by professional organizations. For example, the Editorial Freelancers Association produces a list of the range of rates for a number of different editing services. The rates vary depending on region of the country, your personal experience, and other factors, but quoted ranges can serve as a guideline.

How Much Do You Want to Earn?

Often when setting fees, editors will look at ms complexity and at what other editors are charging, but forget to consider their own income needs. Many new freelance editors think, "I can charge $25 an hour and get enough work to keep me busy 40 hours a week," forgetting that they may need at least $35 an hour to pay their bills.

Start from the position of saying, "I intend to make $X this year" with $X = whatever will pay your rent and keep you in chocolate, plus provide the occasional trip to Disney.

I know I just said you can't be sure how much you'll make when starting out, but this is a theoretical calculation. It's super important, though.

Breaking It Down
I want to make $ _____ this year from my editing.

I will work ____ [number of hours] per week x ____ [number of weeks I plan to work]
= ____ [total number of hours worked]

Note: for general estimating purposes, there are 2,000 work hours in a given year: 40 hours per week multiplied by 50 weeks (you need a little time off!)

Divide the total number of hours worked into the amount of money you want/need/hope to make this year. If the amount you want to make is $50,000 while working 2,000 hours, you need to average $25 per hour. But that's not the end of it.

Because you're self-employed, you have expenses beyond those an employee has. Even if $50,000 sounds like a fair salary, an employee earning $50,000 per year is actually making a lot more than that.

Consider the expenses a self-employed individual has that an employee doesn't have. For example, a staff editor probably has some minimal benefits, such as:

- paid vacation
- paid sick leave
- some portion of health insurance paid; health insurance at lower group rates
- employer contributes the employer's matching portion of money to the Social Security Administration. The freelancer must pay this herself. (It's calculated as part of the Schedule C at income tax time.)
- cost of office space, equipment, supplies, and utilities that the freelancer must provide herself.

In addition—and perhaps most important—you, as a freelancer, are not going to be working on editing projects for every one of those 2,000 hours in your work year. Some of that time is going to be spent marketing your services, and some is going to be spent learning new skills, and some is going to be spent paying your taxes.

In other words, not all of your time is billable, so how much you charge has to account for that.

A staff editor doesn't have to drum up business. If she has to learn a new skill, she gets paid while she's learning it. If she comes down with the flu, she gets paid even though she takes a couple of days off. If there isn't a lot to edit, she still gets paid. (Of course, if there isn't a lot to edit for a long time, she gets laid off and perhaps becomes a freelance editor herself, but that's another story.)

You, on the other hand, will spend a significant percentage of your time finding clients. Freelancers don't get paid for the time they spend developing new business. Also, you'll spend time doing administrative work—buying office supplies, waiting on hold for technical support—that eats up hours and for which you can't bill a client.

To your original hourly figure of $25, add at least 100 percent to cover these costs, creating an adjusted hourly rate. So, using the little template above, we can find that to make $50,000 per year working 2000 hours per year, we'd have to earn $25 an hour. But to make a comparable income to a staffer, we'd really have to earn $50 per hour. That's a big difference.

As you become more expert and don't have to spend as much time marketing your services and can spend more time doing billable work, you'll find that your $50 an hour nets you a salary more similar to someone making $60,000 a year or even more.

You may not end up charging by the hour (and I discourage editors from doing so) but you need to know what your hourly rate is in order to quote projects effectively. In the end, you're selling your time, so you have to be clear in your own mind regarding how much your time is worth.

Once you know that you need to make $50 an hour (for example), then you simply determine how long a project will take and multiply. If you think a project will take ten hours, then you need to charge $500 for the project.

If you're not charging by the hour and therefore won't be compensated if you exceed your estimated amount of time, you'll need to be sure that you're estimating your time correctly. Quoting a project for $500 doesn't work out very well if it ends up taking you thirty hours to do the work.

Once you know how much you need to charge you can quote fees in different ways—by the hour, by the project, etc.

By the Hour, Page, Word, or Project?

Let's look at the different ways of charging a bit more in-depth. Which of the approaches is in your best interest?

The answer, as in so much about freelancing, is "it depends." Each has benefits and drawbacks.

Hourly Fees

Pros: Being paid by the hour means you'll be compensated for all of the time you spend on an editing project. Whether it takes you five hours or fifty, you're paid for the hours you work.

Cons: As you become better at editing, it takes you less time to complete a given project, so you actually get paid less for your expertise. If the rate is $50 an hour and a beginner takes three hours and an expert takes two, the beginner makes more money, which hardly seems fair. Some of this disadvantage can be offset by charging a higher hourly fee—but clients looking just at hourly rates may decide yours are too high.

You may find that clients balk at hourly fees unless they can put an upper-limit cap on the hours, which means you're basically offering a project fee (and which largely eliminates the major advantage of this approach, which is to be compensated for your time however long it takes).

Per Page/Per Word Fees

Pros: You get paid for each word/page you edit, regardless of how long it takes you to edit it. If you go faster, you still get paid the agreed-upon amount. The client knows exactly how much the edit will cost ahead of time.

Cons: If it takes a long time to edit each page, you may not be compensated fairly. This can happen if you charge everyone the same flat per-word/page fee or if the sample pages you've reviewed have been polished by the author but the rest of the manuscript has not. One drawback from the client's perspective is concern that you may try to speed through the project, sacrificing quality.

Project Fees

Pros: You get paid the fee no matter how long the edit takes. If you can edit quickly, this can result in a higher profit margin. This approach eliminates arguments over the amount of your hourly fee and how long you will take to do the edit and it allows you to account for the complexity of the edit (unlike per-word/page fees). You can also customize the edit to the client's needs without losing income—you can fold in charges for launch meetings and answering client questions without having to charge those as separate line items. Additionally, clients like to know that one price will cover the entire cost of editing.

Cons: If the project runs into snags, you may spend more time on it than you're being compensated for. As with per-page fees, if the sample pages you've reviewed have been polished but the rest of the ms has not, you may find yourself spending more time editing than you expected. (You can mostly eliminate this problem by reviewing the entire ms before taking on a project.)

My Recommendations Regarding Fees

If I'm doing something fairly standard, like a developmental edit for a publisher, I always quote a project fee because clients prefer to know exactly what they're getting and for what price. As I mentioned above, I don't use per-word or per-page fees because the quality of manuscripts can vary so much. A project fee lets me tailor the quote to the project. It also means I don't have to defend how many hours I think the project will take to edit or my hourly fee.

For more open-ended projects, like working with a client on her query letter, I charge a coaching fee, which is an hourly rate. I give the author a sense of how long a task will take and bill the actual time spent. If I'm likely to go over my estimate by a significant amount (more than 10 percent or so) I'll let the author know ahead of time and we'll work out a solution.

This piecemeal approach allows an author to come to me with small projects and requests (such as help brainstorming) that don't require the effort of a complete manuscript assessment and project quote.

For standard projects like a developmental edit, I always let clients know that I can do work outside the scope of the agreement (for example, a second round of revisions, or a conference call with a coauthor) at my regular coaching fee of $X per hour, and I let them know when we've reached the point where I will have to start charging it. This helps me keep control over how much time it takes to do a project while giving the client options should they need additional help.

Client-Set Fees

Some corporate clients (book publishers/packagers) prefer to pay per-page fees or per-word fees and have set rates for this. You get paid for each page/word you edit, regardless of how long it takes you to edit it. If it takes you two minutes to edit a page, you get paid the agreed-upon amount for that page, even though you whizzed right through it.

The con, of course, is if it takes a long time to edit each page, you may not be compensated fairly. If you're good and quick and the project doesn't have major structural problems that require a lot of work for you to identify and provide solutions for, then you can come out pretty well.

But if there are a lot of big-picture concerns to deal with and an author who needs a lot of direction, then it can turn out to be the kind of thing where you're better off flipping burgers at McDonald's.

Remember that even though corporations may have set rates they pay, these are not written in stone. It's always worth negotiating. Always ask for more —

whether that's more money or more time or more of whatever you want. Often you'll get it.

Client-set fees are usually established in a pay range, and the first figure quoted will be on the low end of the range. Ask for twenty to thirty percent more. Ask for twenty to thirty percent more even if the client offers a decent amount. You'll probably get something. If not, you can always agree to the first figure. It's not as if the client is going to withdraw the offer. (Repeat to yourself, "This is my job, this is how I earn a living, I deserve to earn a decent wage.")

Always be polite and courteous. You don't need to buckle at the first sound of hesitation but you don't need to destroy a potentially lucrative relationship, either. Counter the first offer, consider the counter-offer if there is one, and make a decision. Be polite but firm regardless of what you decide.

More Money, Fewer Clients

So far, most of my focus has been on editors who are newly establishing their businesses. But there may come a time when you aren't looking for more clients — you're booked up. Instead, you're looking for ways to make more money.

Obviously one way to do this is to work faster and book more clients, but that ends up being a crazy treadmill. There's a limit to how fast you can work and still produce quality results. So, there are better ways for you to increase your income.

Trade Up

Try trading up—finding clients who'll pay more for your expertise than the clients you currently have.

Freelancers often assume more is better—more marketing equals more clients—but this isn't necessarily the case. Targeting your marketing efforts more specifically can often produce better results than blanketing the world indiscriminately with your message.

One of the most important ways to do this is to listen carefully to the feedback you get and to adjust your approach. "I only hire editors who have worked on traditionally published books" may sound like another frustrating turndown, but it's actually valuable information. If this potential client wants to see traditionally published books on your editorial resume, then it's likely others do, too, and this is why you're not getting the responses you'd like.

What could you do to get a traditionally published book or two on your resume? Who do you know who can help you make that happen?

Here's another example. One publisher I was interested in working for doesn't hire editors who are also writers. I don't know why they have this policy but when companies have such policies, I don't try to change the policy ("But I'm different from every other writer slash editor you've worked with!") or lie about it ("Why, no, I'm not a writer. All those books you see on Amazon belong to some other Jennifer Lawler"). I just move along. Don't waste time on leads that don't lead anywhere.

I happened to mention this publisher to an editor friend of mine who isn't also a writer and she was thrilled to apply.

When you're trading up, your colleagues are an invaluable source of information. They often know going rates publishers and packagers pay or know the names of people you can pitch at the next step up.

In general, smaller publishers have smaller budgets and larger companies have larger budgets, though this is not universally true. So, if you're currently getting work from smaller publishing companies, it might be time to move up the food chain.

One caveat: the largest publishing companies don't hire many freelance developmental editors. They do hire freelance CEs and proofreaders — but you will face considerable competition, so you have to have good skills.

When working with indie clients, you can gradually increase your rates — say, 10 percent per year — and still retain most of them. If you're undervaluing your services, though, it can take a while to get up to par. You may have to market to a different client base to make big jumps in fees. Go back to Chapter 1 to consider ways to revise your purpose that can open up a more lucrative client base.

Offer a Variety of Services

Most successful freelancers offer a variety of related services in a variety of price ranges to accommodate for potential clients' needs, including budget. This helps ensure you're not letting potential income slip through your fingers. If you're a developmental editor, and you charge (this is a completely made-up number!) $2000 to develop a 60,000 word novel, you probably have some potential clients who can't pay that fee.

If you can offer a related, but less time-consuming and therefore less expensive, service then you could potentially convert some of those can't-afford-it people into paying clients. For example, maybe you can offer a critique, which is just a read-through of the ms with your notes regarding any major issues you encountered. Maybe this takes eight or ten hours instead of sixty (or more!) required for the DE. You would reduce your fee accordingly.

You might also consider offering other budget-friendly options such as review of the first three chapters instead of the entire ms (most dev problems will crop up early on anyway). Or, teach a group class on revision or write (and sell!) a book on common mistakes newer writers make. The benefit of less expensive items like a book or a class is that they introduce potential clients to you without requiring an expensive investment right off.

On the higher end of the scale, if you have potential clients who need more hand-holding throughout the process, you could do coaching, which is any kind of one-on-one teaching, such as brainstorming with the author as she tries to create a stronger central conflict for her WIP, helping the author storyboard her new book concept, creating writing prompts to help the client develop stronger skills in certain areas, and so on.

For clients who don't need development, maybe you can do copyediting or proofreading (bear in mind that no one editor should perform all these tasks on one ms;

the editorial process requires more than one set of eyes on a ms to make sure it is error-free).

Create Low-, Middle-, and High-End Services

A fun brain fact is that buyers who have three options will quite likely choose the middle option. So, think in terms of having a budget option, a regular option, and a luxury option. People will likely choose the regular (middle) option (so make sure it's the one where you make the most profit!)

If you have only low-end services, it's hard to be profitable; it takes a lot of time and effort to get enough clients coming through the door—not to mention the time and effort it takes to do a lot of edits. If you have only high-end offerings, it may be a long drought between clients. For most freelance editors, then, a variety of choices is going to be more likely to result in a profitable business.

Another approach would be to offer people who take the low-end deal the opportunity to apply some or all of the price to the high-end deal (assuming that's possible/makes sense). This is one way to convert customers who aren't completely sure what they're getting into. For example, people who buy your book can get a small discount on your class. People who take your class get a discount on your editing services.

Acquiring Complementary Skills

In addition to offering a menu of services, it doesn't hurt to acquire complementary skills. For example, maybe in addition to DE, you can also review queries, synopses, and book proposals. These require specialized knowledge (to know what agents and acquisitions editors are looking for), but if you have it, or can get it, you can open up more possibilities. Or, if you have some expertise in ebook formatting or book promotion, these are complementary skills that clients might be interested in.

You can acquire additional skills in many different ways. Some people are self-taught. Others find a mentor who can show them the ropes. Online (or in-person) classes from professional organizations are a great resource.

Show Your Flexibility

As I have already described, specializing in a certain niche helps you identify and market in that niche (much easier to do and generally more lucrative than trying to be a generalist—all things to all people). It's going to be easier to find clients if everyone knows that you're an awesome cookbook editor. But don't be afraid of letting potential clients know that you're flexible.

It helps attract clients if you can say, "Yes, I've edited nine cookbooks," but it also helps if you can say, "Yes, I edit mostly cookbooks, but I also edit how-to and most kinds of nonfiction." Notice that "flexibility" means "closely related skills" not "a bunch of completely unrelated activities."

You may need to brush up on some skills to do this, but it allows you access to different potentially lucrative markets, it helps prevent you from getting bored by doing the same thing over and over, and it gives you flexibility should one source of business dry up. It also helps you explore different areas that you might also like to specialize in.

Build a Partnership

One way to broaden your reach is to work with other freelancers to mutually market each other's work. I mean moving beyond "I'll send referrals your way if you send referrals mine" to something more formal. For example, maybe you and a colleague pitch a client a complete editorial package — you'll do the developmental edit and your colleague will do the copyedit.

A one-time project such as this doesn't involve much risk because you're not committing your entire career or your entire business to the partnership. But because they're so simple, they tend to be casual and informal, which can lead to misunderstandings. Be certain that each partner's duty on a project is carefully laid out and that all partners communicate regularly with each other.

Business Partnerships

More complex partnerships are business-oriented, not project-oriented. You and another person with similar or complementary skills decide to go into business together, or you decide to take someone into business with you.

Partnerships are more challenging to do well if you both have the same skills—for example, if both of you are developmental editors. However, these partnerships can sometimes work, especially if you have related but not the same specialties: One of you specializes in women's fiction and the other in memoir. Or, they can succeed if each of you focuses on different aspects of the business, such as one of you doing the marketing and admin (recruiting clients, sending invoices) and the other working on the editorial end (delivering the work).

If you're considering a partnership, spend some time with the potential partner first, such as by doing a trial project together, before committing fully. When you participate in this trial run, don't remain on your best behavior. Try to see how you and your partner handle stress, division of responsibility, and deadlines. If the potential partner is a friend, be especially careful: is it worth losing the friend if the partnership doesn't work out?

Define Specifics Early

Clearly define your partnership up front. If you want someone to assist you in the business but you want to remain in control, you don't want a partnership, you want a good employee (and there's nothing wrong with that). Recognize what you want and what you're willing to give up for it.

If you and another person intend to have equal say in the running of the partnership or if you both plan to be part owners of the business, you need to enter into a legal partnership agreement that specifies what each of you provides and what each of you receives. Be clear about this from the beginning to avoid problems later on.

Who will be in control day-to-day? What if the partners disagree on the direction the company is taking? What if the personal circumstances of one partner change and that partner can no longer (or no longer wants to) continue operating in the same capacity?

Circumstances that can dramatically change the nature of a partnership include one of the partners marrying or divorcing, having a child, or becoming ill or injured. What will you do if something like this occurs? Consider how to dissolve, sell, or terminate the partnership.

Discuss the purpose of your business and what each partner will do. Work out your arrangements in detail. Although a lawyer can alert you to potential pitfalls in your plans, you should be the ones making the plans. The lawyer should merely formalize the partnership agreement.

Examine your temperament and honestly assess your personality. Would you make a good partner? In a partnership, the risks and burdens are shared. But being scared to go it alone is not a good enough reason to enter into a partnership.

It's essential to spend time talking about the business, weighing concerns, researching, and investigating the idea before actually committing to a partnership. I've had some good partnerships and some go terribly wrong. A few book collaborations have been very successful, whereas one or two "Let's combine our talents and create a content empire" forays never got very far. Over time, I've realized I don't have the right temperament for long-term partnerships.

Transition Your Business

A great many freelancers build a business doing one type of work—say, copyediting—and that's fine, but over time they identify other related areas where they could be making more money. For example, editing nonfiction for professionals pays better than editing fiction for indie authors; technical editing pays better than general nonfiction editing; developmental editing pays better than copyediting; coaching/consulting pays better than both.

So maybe you decide you'd like to transition at least some of your business from copyediting to developmental editing or that you'd like some of your developmental editing work to be nonfiction instead fiction.

Or maybe you're not concerned about money so much as you care about doing work you enjoy, so maybe you decide you'd like to transition from copyediting nonfiction to copyediting fiction.

To develop a business that includes a related but different skill, you have to build bridges from one to the other. You can do this by taking advantage of opportunities that naturally arise, such as when a copyediting client asks, "Can you do development on this project in our pipeline?"

You may hesitate if you haven't done this for pay before but if the client trusts you, you feel you have the necessary skills, and you're careful to understand and communicate expectations, you're likely to do just fine. And then you'll have experience that you can use to garner more of the same type of work.

If no one conveniently asks you to do developmental editing when you've only done copyediting for them before, you can ask them. You can say something like, "I'm transitioning into doing more developmental editing and I'd love to be considered for such projects." Or "I'm now doing developmental editing for fiction as well as nonfiction. Would you be willing to let any of your colleagues know that I'm available for this?"

Or, you can turn a current problem into an opportunity: "Client, for these three reasons, this new project you sent me really requires a round of development before it goes to copyedit. I'd be happy to do the development for you."

However, it's likely that you will have to go beyond your current clients to establish a change in direction. Even so, start where you are now and with who you know now. How do you get from here to where you want to be? Who can help you get there? What do you need to do to make the transition easier?

For example, would taking classes help you feel more confident about the new work? Or joining a different set of organizations? Maybe you could try attending a conference targeted toward your new audience/clientele.

Make sure your website indicates this change. Call it an "additional service" or a "new offering." You can even send out a newsletter to your clients (and/or a press release to local media) about the change.

You're not starting completely from scratch but you are, in many ways, starting over. Embrace that! Don't get too caught up in the way you already do things. Be open to new opportunities and new learning experiences.

Your Personal Financial Future

Your personal financial future is intimately connected with your business. If your business is successful, you'll be able to save money, put the kids through college, and retire before you're eighty-two. But this will happen only if you prepare for it. It won't happen by accident or because you net a million dollars a year as an editor.

Many freelancers make the mistake of investing all their time and effort into their business without taking other steps to care for their own financial future. In fact, they often jeopardize their own financial future by using personal credit cards for the business or investing all of their savings in the business.

They reason that if the business is successful enough, it will pay for their needs. Or maybe they hope that at some point they'll sell the business and retire on the profits.

Have Realistic Expectations

"Sell the business and retire on the proceeds" isn't going to work for you. (Or at least probably not.) As a freelance editor, you are your business. Once you're gone, there is no business. The exception might be if you have a child or partner who could take over, or if your business produces a product that someone could continue to make/sell after you're gone, such as a book.

But for the most part, you're not going to be able to sell your business when you're sixty-five and retire on the proceeds.

So you need to be clear-eyed about what how your business is doing. If it's limping along, can you do something to make it more financially viable? Or would you be better off getting a staff job and perhaps continuing with freelancing as a side hustle?

Personal Finances Affect Business Decisions

Personal financial problems can adversely affect your business. If you don't have enough personal savings to cover the cost of a new furnace in your home, you may make poor business decisions, like steeply discounting your services in order to get the necessary money. This may work in the short-term but in the long-term it teaches your clients that they should only pay your steeply discounted rate.

For this reason, it's important to know where the pain points in your personal financial life are going to be. If you know you're going to need to purchase a new car in the next few years, and you have absolutely no way to save for that outlay right now, you need to assess whether there are actions you can take that won't be ultimately harmful or disruptive to your business in order to start saving for that expense.

In broader terms, your personal financial goals will always affect how you run your business. Every few months—at least once a year—you should consider what your future needs will be and reassess any plans and goals that you've already set. You may have children you want to put through college. You may want to retire while you're still young enough to travel. Can your business support these goals?

Along with the goals you want to reach, you need to consider what you'll do if things don't work out the way you planned—for instance, if you become disabled. Once you've identified the issues of personal financial concern, you need to consider how you'll meet your needs. (Chapter 7 discusses insurance, including life and disability insurance.)

Saving for Uncertainty

As your business becomes profitable, you must set aside a certain amount for savings because the unexpected invariably happens just when you're having trouble getting your clients to pay. Most financial planners recommend having readily accessible savings (money under the mattress) equivalent to two to six month's income.

For freelancers, readily accessible savings should include business operating expenses as well as personal living expenses. You need to save more than two months' income, since it can take time to restart the business that you've had to shut down while recuperating from an unexpected illness or something similar.

Beyond the emergency savings, money should be set aside in a retirement fund. Since you don't have an employer anymore, you won't have an employer-funded retirement program to take care of you. With current concerns about the viability of the social security system, it's probably not a good idea to decide you'll rely on that in your old age.

Although you may want to help your kids pay for college, most experts recommend that you take care of your retirement first. As they point out, you or your child can take out student loans, but you can't take out loans to see you through retirement.

You can pay some college expenses out of your income when the time comes. Your kids can help pay for college by taking jobs during the summer or working part-time during the school year. Government grants (which you don't have to pay back) are also available.

A combination of these different tactics can be used to put your child through college. But if you haven't looked after yourself, you'll still be working when you're eighty-two.

Chapter 6

The Paperwork Part: Setting Up Your Business

So far, I've encouraged you not to overcomplicate your efforts. You don't need to sign up for the $99-per-month Basecamp subscription or take out expensive ads in writers' magazines before you have your first client. Keep it simple.

The reason I encourage this (besides the fact that you may never need Basecamp or ads) is because many would-be freelancers believe running a freelancing business is actually more complicated than it is. Many are afraid to strike out on their own because the details seem overwhelming—Estimated taxes! Business licenses! Zoning laws!

Relax. If you can edit a full-length manuscript without losing your marbles, you've got this. The problem is that most people sensibly fall asleep when subjects as boring as "accounting programs" and "contractual liability" come up. Although it is not possible to make those topics interesting, I promise to introduce you to them as painlessly as I can.

If you're contemplating starting a small business (which is basically what you'll be doing if you begin freelancing), you'll discover — or may already have discovered — that most of what is written about business ownership has absolutely nothing to do with you. Business books and articles spend a lot of time talking about training employees and finding your successor as CEO. And I've already covered the useless margaritas-on-the-beach people.

A lot of what's written about business ownership makes the entire concept of business ownership seem alien, unattainable, and fraught with danger. But business ownership isn't hard. At least, it isn't hard the way analytical calculus is hard. Business ownership is hard because it requires hard work. But it isn't alien, unattainable, or even very much fraught with danger.

Note that what I'm about to say here applies to US-based businesses only, but similar considerations are true wherever you work. I'm not a lawyer or a CPA, nor am I in the business of giving legal or accounting advice. The information provided here is general information. I have tried to be accurate but make no promises or guarantees. Consult with the appropriate experts to be sure you're following your federal and local laws and rules governing business operations.

Types of Business Ownership

One of the first decisions you'll make is to decide the form of business organization you intend to run. Since you're almost certainly doing this with a profit motive, I'll limit my discussion to the most common forms of for-profit business structures.

Sole Proprietorship

If you are a freelancer with no partners in the business, then you run a sole proprietorship. There's just you and the cat and the cat does not materially participate. A sole proprietorship is the least complicated type of business to own but it has some drawbacks. A business with a single proprietor (owner) is closely linked to the proprietor's personal wealth (or lack thereof). If your business gets sued, you get sued. If your business goes bankrupt, guess what? There's no way to protect your personal assets should a financial loss occur in connection with your business. Your spouse's assets and earnings are also at risk (provided you have a spouse with assets and earnings).

But a sole proprietorship is very easy to handle at tax time. Several special forms are used, but the taxes are simply part of your personal income tax. You don't file separately for your business. (Tax issues are discussed later in Chapter 7). You typically don't have to license or register a sole proprietorship, with certain exceptions that almost never apply to editors, making start-up a snap.

General Partnership

A general partnership is a business with two or more principal partners. The cat is optional. The partners, called general partners, agree on each person's financial responsibility, each person's duties, and each person's compensation. A general partnership, like a sole proprietorship, doesn't protect the owners from business-related lawsuits. If one partner gets sued while acting in any capacity for the business, the other partner is equally at risk. Since personal wealth and income are not protected, the spouses of partners can be affected by a lawsuit or bankruptcy.

Partnerships are commonly used when one person has an idea and another has the financial backing for it, but they are sometimes used when two or more people with complementary skills decide to go into business together.

Some states require partnerships to register and further require the parties to have a written agreement outlining the details of the partnership. States that don't require an agreement assume a 50-50 split of revenue (money earned) and expenses (money spent). (You need a written agreement to do otherwise).

Beyond this, a separate bank account in the name of the partnership is required and special tax documents must be filed with the federal, state, and local governments. Any taxes due are owed by the individuals, however, and appear on each partner's individual income tax returns. This keeps the tax recordkeeping simpler than for other business organizations with more than one owner.

Corporations

You can also incorporate your business, which can be expensive and time-consuming. Corporations limit or reduce a business owner's liability. The personal wealth of the owner(s) is not at stake, with the exception of anything he or she actually invested in the business. Therefore, if someone sues the company, the company and its profits could be lost, but the personal wealth of the owners (such as your house) would not be at stake. The corporation itself is recognized as a separate entity, just like a person, in the eyes of the government.

Three main types of corporations exist: C corporations, subchapter S corporations, and limited liability corporations.

C corporations must file separate income tax statements and pay corporate income taxes. Owners are paid salaries or dividends that are further taxed as their personal income. For this reason, C corporations make profits that are double-taxed. Only large companies or those with complicated ownership issues need to be registered as C corporations.

Subchapter S corporations allow the owners to record income on their personal income tax statements and so avoid double taxation. Most small business owners can incorporate as S corporations.

Recent tax law changes make deciding between a C or S corporation structure more complex than formerly, so do talk with an adviser before making any final decisions.

Limited liability corporations (sometimes called limited liability companies), also limit the owners' potential liability and have many similarities to a partnership. The liability of the partners is limited to whatever they have invested in the business. Like an S corporation, a limited liability corporation (LLC) allows business income to be reported on the owners' personal income tax statement, thus avoiding double taxation. An LLC allows different owners to share in the profits differently, which cannot be done with an S corporation.

All three types of corporations require registration with the state and federal government, a written agreement among owners, special separate income tax returns, separate business bank accounts, and slightly more complicated recordkeeping.

All partnerships and corporations must obtain an Employer Identification Number (called, not very originally, an EIN) from the federal government. This number appears on tax and payroll paperwork. Even if the business has no employees, the number is required.

If you run a sole proprietorship and you employ others, you must also request an EIN. (If you run a sole proprietorship and it's just you and the cat, you don't need an EIN—you can use your own social security number). An EIN can be obtained by using IRS Form SS-4, Application for Employer Identification Number. You can apply online at **www.irs.gov**.

Additional Considerations

Although the idea of protecting yourself from lawsuits is appealing, incorporating doesn't necessarily protect your personal wealth. Why not? Because being the owner of a corporation or LLC does not prevent you from being sued under professional liability laws. Professional liability means that people in certain professions—such as physicians, lawyers, writers—are personally responsible for the actions and outcomes that occur when they practice their profession, regardless of the form of the business they own and regardless of by whom they are employed.

A writer can be personally sued for plagiarism or copyright infringement regardless of the type of business she runs. If she is found guilty, her business, home, and personal assets can all be lost. This is pertinent if any part of your business involves ghostwriting or coauthorship.

For an editor, the risks are slimmer — a mistake you make in an edit isn't likely to lead to such dire outcomes. Note that editors working for publishing companies have been personally named in lawsuits dealing with intellectual property, so you will want to understand your risks. A conversation with a good intellectual property lawyer in your area will help you make appropriate decisions about how to protect yourself. (One such way is with professional liability insurance — more on insurance in Chapter 7.)

Incorporating may make sense if your company will employ other people or if it will own land or expensive equipment. If you employ someone to run errands for your company, and that person is involved in an auto accident on the way to the office supply store, your company can be sued.

If your company is a corporation, the amount you could lose is limited to your business. Professional liability would not be an issue in a case like this, since having an accident while buying paper clips is not the same as publishing defamatory statements about the shift manager at the hardware store.

If you need a bank loan for your business, you may be required to form a corporation in order to protect the bank's financial liability. Some freelancers who do contract work for corporations find they get paid faster as a corporation than as an individual.

You can change the form of your business as it grows and evolves. You may begin as a sole proprietor, then decide to take on a partner and form a partnership. Then as your business grows and you hire an assistant, you might decide to form a corporation. Or if you begin a partnership and your partner doesn't hold up his or her end of the deal, you can become a sole proprietor. Consult an experienced small business attorney to learn more about the pros and cons of each type of business ownership.

Your Company Name

You can give your business a name even if you run a sole proprietorship. You don't have to incorporate to use a "doing business as" name (also called a "dba"). All you have to do is register the fictitious name, usually with the state and the city clerk. This requires a small fee. Some states and localities don't even require the registration of a fictitious name.

If you do use a fictitious name as a sole proprietor, you can't call your company an LLC or a corporation or put "Inc." somewhere in the name. Beyond that, practically anything is acceptable. If your clients will be locals, that's probably all you need to worry about doing.

For complete protection of your company name, however, you can file for trademark registration with the federal (and/or state) government. Minions will conduct what amounts to a title search and if no other company has the name, you'll be allowed to trademark it. This means that if someone else uses your company's name, you can send them mean letters telling them to stop.

Applying to trademark your company name prevents you from using a company name belonging to someone else—you'll be notified if the name you've chosen is already protected. That way, you won't receive a letter six years down the road saying you have to change the name of your company or prepare to defend a lawsuit. This can happen even if you used the name first, if you didn't register it first.

The drawback, of course, is that trademark registration takes time and costs several hundred dollars. (Those minions are expensive.) It may be worthwhile if you'll have clients from across the country and it's possible that your company name could become widely known.

You can apply for trademark registration at any time; it doesn't have to be done the second you open your business. (I applied for trademark registration once for a series of book titles and was granted the trademark; the process was time-consuming but the minions were very friendly and readily answered my questions.)

Special Business Requirements

You'll need to learn about any special requirements your city and state has for businesses. For small business rules and regulations, the local office of the Small Business Administration (SBA) is as good place to start as any. The first thing they always (always!) ask is if you have a business plan, regardless of what you want to know. Tell them you're researching it, which is why you're talking to them. Much of their information applies to manufacturing or service businesses with employees so you will have to make them focus on your particular issues instead of letting them tell you what you would do if you were going to open a chemical processing plant.

Zoning Laws

Most residential areas have zoning laws prohibiting people from operating businesses from their homes. Such laws are intended to prevent neighborhood blight and security problems (garish signs, increased traffic, delivery trucks blocking access, people coming and going at unseemly hours). The idea is that the suburbs should stay pristine and unsullied by crass commercialism.

For an editor who conducts most business by email, zoning laws aren't a big deal. If you have clients coming to meet you, this could pose a bigger problem. To address potential problems, try to maintain friendly relations with your neighbors and your neighborhood association. Be willing to reach compromises. Perhaps you could meet some of your clients at a nearby coffee shop or tell them that as an added service, you will visit them. Know local zoning ordinances because being in violation of them is hard on your wallet and can even put you out of business.

Business License

Check local ordinances to learn if you need a business license to operate your type of business. Business licenses are usually readily available for a small fee. Call city hall or the city clerk and ask for guidelines for small business owners and home-based business owners.

Sales Tax Collection

If you sell a product, such as a book, you'll (probably) need to collect state, county, and local sales tax and turn it over to the appropriate government offices. Professional services, such as editing a manuscript, are generally exempt from sales tax (but not in all areas). To collect and remit sales tax, contact the city clerk, county clerk, and state treasurer, since each will have different reporting requirements (in some places the state collects all sales tax and doles it out to the city and county but this is not universal).

Usually you have to register your business, be given a sales tax number, and file a report monthly, quarterly, or annually, depending on how much tax you will be collecting. The SBA also has advice on collecting and remitting sales taxes.

Business Taxes

If your community imposes property taxes on personal property such as furniture or computers, your business will owe business taxes on its assets (the things it owns). Check with your local tax assessor to determine what you need to do to pay these taxes.

Keeping Good Financial Records

The key to not going broke as a freelancer is knowing where your money is coming from and where it's going. Recordkeeping helps you keep track. It's also necessary for income tax purposes.

Many freelancers think they can just hire an accountant to figure out their financial information and keep the records. But I don't recommend that. You know those millionaire celebrities who died broke? They all had accountants.

It's up to you to keep control over financial decision-making in your life and in your business. You can't do this if someone else is in charge of the financial information or if you don't understand the financial information.

Even if ultimately you decide to leave all the accounting to your accountant, unless you make an effort to understand the basics, you'll never understand what your accountant is telling you or why it's important.

It's impossible to overstate how crucial the financial picture of your business is, even if it seems crass and coldhearted to spend all that time focusing on money.

The purpose of financial recordkeeping is to help you understand if you're making a living or not. Although financial records are necessary to please the IRS and to convince financial institutions to lend you money if you need some, most importantly, these financial records are for you. If you don't use them, you'll never understand why you're working so hard and still can't afford to buy shoes.

Cash or Accrual?

In order to keep accurate financial records, you must decide whether to operate your business on a cash or accrual basis. A cash basis business records revenue when it is received and records expenditures when they are paid. (It has nothing to do with whether you accept cash, checks, or credit cards.)

If I'm running a cash-basis business and on Monday, February 4th, I purchase a ream of copy paper, six pens, and a dictionary for a total of $45.38 (tax included), and in the mail, lo and behold, I receive a check for $250 for a small editing job I did, my expenses for the day will be $45.38 and my income will be $250. That's it.

Freelancers generally rely on the cash basis accounting system. Their business finances are no more complex than getting money for their work and spending some of it on business needs.

However, sometimes smaller businesses use the accrual basis instead of the cash basis system because of the complexity of their financial calculations. The accrual basis system records income and expenses when they are incurred (or accrued), not when they are paid. This gives business owners a better picture of what their financial situation really is, because it records their financial commitments.

The accrual basis accounting system always requires adjustments. Suppose you bill a client on Monday, February 4, a total of $1000 and offer a ten percent discount if the bill is paid within fifteen days. You will immediately record the $1000 as income or revenue, even though you haven't got the money in your hand.

Now, if your client never pays you, at some later date you will record a "bad debt" expense of $1000 to balance out that fact that you already recorded the $1000 as revenue. You're still out the $1000 that your client owes you, but the accounting system is happy. (A cash-basis business can't write off bad debt because it never said that the money was received.)

Suppose, on the other hand, that the company pays your $1000 invoice within fifteen days. Because the client paid promptly, the check is for $900, which is ten percent off the $1000 bill. To account for this, since you already recorded $1000 as revenue, you will indicate an expense of $100 as a discount. (A cash-basis business, on the other hand, would simply show revenue of $900 when the check was received.)

The accrual basis system provides more information. You could learn that discounting costs your business thousands of dollars each year, so perhaps you should cut back on the number of clients you offer the discount to, reduce the amount of the discount, eliminate it entirely, or raise your prices. Each solution has its own problems but if you used the cash-basis system you might never know how much discounting costs you.

If you're a sole proprietor, you should use the cash-basis accounting system (in most cases, the IRS will require it). There are some exceptions, such as if you need complex financial documents, your business is involved in complex financial arrangements, you maintain an inventory, or you must track depreciation (the loss of value of goods, such as computers and cars, that happens over time). These do not apply to most editorial freelancers. Many general partnerships can also operate using the cash-basis system as can some corporations.

You must establish your method of accounting before you put your business into operation because once you've decided on an accounting basis, you cannot change it without considerable trial and tribulation. The IRS, from whom you must get permission to make a change, will punish you by making you fill out twelve or eighteen forms and then losing them.

The Balance Sheet

Accountants like to make balance sheets, which show the assets and liabilities of a business (that which is owned and that which is owed). In accounting, assets (things you own) are called debits while liabilities (things you owe) are called credits. If you get a migraine trying to remember which is which, just record things as assets or liabilities and forget which is a credit and which is a debit.

Now if you and I wanted to figure out what we owned and what we owed, we would make a list of revenues and total it and then make a list of expenses and total it and then we would look at the two lists and decide if something needed to be done. We would be happy with that. And then we would get on with our lives.

Accountants are not so easy to please. They want both sides of the lists, assets and liabilities, to total the same amount — to balance. They will go to bizarre and unhealthy ends to make this happen.

Here's what you need to know: *assets* (what you own) always equal *liabilities* (what you owe) plus *capital* (equity or ownership interest). Capital is, in effect, the difference between assets and liabilities. It's put there to make both sides of a balance sheet balance.

Well, it serves another purpose, which is to show whether the business itself has worth. If the capital number is negative, that's a bad thing. It means you owe more than the business is worth. If the capital number is positive, then you're on the right track. Probably.

How does this work? In the beginning, the business is an idea in your mind. There is nothing tangible to it. Then you take a computer that you've had sitting around the den and designate it the business computer. You add a hundred dollars from your Christmas bonus to buy a bookshelf. Now you have assets of computer and bookshelf on one side of the equation, and capital (the amount the computer and bookshelf are worth) on the other side of the equation.

If you then charge fifty dollars' worth of books to your credit card, you would have assets of a computer, bookshelf, and books, and liabilities in the amount of the credit card charge. The difference between the worth of the assets and the amount of the liabilities is the net worth of your business, or the owner's interest, equity, or capital, which all mean basically the same thing.

If your net worth is a positive number, it means that you could sell your assets and pay off your liabilities and still have money left over for pizza. If your net worth is a negative number, it means that if you sell your assets and use the money to pay your liabilities, you would still owe money to creditors after all your assets are gone.

The balance sheet is a helpful financial document because it shows the health of your business. If what you owe is much greater than what you own, your business could be in serious trouble. If the opposite is true, enjoy your three-week Caribbean vacation because you've earned it.

One system of daily recordkeeping essentially mimics a balance sheet. Using this method, you keep track of both sides of the balance sheet on a day-to-day basis. This type of recordkeeping is called "double entry bookkeeping."

Only if you are insane, extremely anal, or in a complex financial arrangement do you need to bother driving yourself nuts with double entry bookkeeping. Instead, you will simply keep a general ledger using single entry bookkeeping.

The General Ledger

If your business operates on a cash basis, you don't need to worry about recording depreciation and bad debt. You don't need to worry about your balance sheet on a daily basis. Keep it simple. Use a general ledger.

Fine, you say, now if only I knew what a general ledger was. A general ledger resembles a checkbook register, noting income and expenses.

In the ledger — which can be kept using a notebook, a computer program, or a sheet of bark — you write the account information for every financial transaction that occurs in your business. An *account* is the name for an entry in the accounting record. The account should show the amount of revenue or expense, the date it was paid, who paid it or was paid, the reason for the income or expense, and the category of revenue or expense.

Account Categories

Using account categories is just a way to group similar items together. Throughout the year, you may buy pens, notebooks, and folders. These are the supplies you need to run your business. You might categorize all such expenses as "supplies." In addition, you might advertise on Facebook and in a writers' magazine. These expenses could be lumped together under "advertising."

Revenue includes income that clients pay you, plus special income from one-time sales (such as selling a computer you've replaced), as well as interest earned on investments. Using these categories helps you understand where your money comes from and where it goes. You might see that you spend a great deal of money on supplies. You can then find a cheaper supplier, quit being so wasteful, or choose different quality materials.

Most business owners use account types that match the account categories the IRS uses, such as "advertising expense" and "professional fees." These are listed on the Schedule C form. Recording business expenses under the account type that the IRS allows makes it easier when it comes time to file tax returns.

Loans and Loan Payments

Remember that loans are not revenue and loan payments are not expenses (although interest payments are expenses), at least not in the bookkeeping sense. Some business owners make this mistake, which inflates their income incorrectly and increases the amount of taxes they have to pay. It also inflates their expenses incorrectly, which can cause tax problems down the road. The money from a loan is an asset (something you own), while the repayment obligation for the loan is a liability (something you owe), but loans and loan payments do not officially belong in a cash-basis general ledger, which only tracks revenue and expenses.

If you have loans and loan payments, record them on a balance sheet, not the general ledger. If you have large loans, complex repayment schedules, or other tricky financial situations, you should consult with an accountant to determine how to set up an appropriate accounting system.

Income Statement (Profit-and-Loss Statement)

Once you have established a general ledger for your daily revenue and expense information, you can generate helpful reports. The income statement, also known as the profit-and-loss statement, is one of these helpful reports. It can be used to look at financial records over the course of a week, a month, a year — any amount of time you care to use. The general ledger itself provides the information about revenue and expenses for the period of time in which you're interested.

An income statement simply totals your revenue and your expenses. Expenses are subtracted from revenue to determine net income. Knowing your net income for a given period of time allows you to see how much money your business actually generates. If your net income is a negative number, watch out! You're operating at a loss, which can cause your business to fail.

Most of these reports can be automatically generated using accounting software like Quicken.

Accounts Payable and Accounts Receivable

Accounts payable is money you owe or will owe in the near future and accounts receivable is the money owed to you. Because the cash-basis accounting system doesn't record income until the money is actually in the bank, and it doesn't consider expenses until they are actually paid, the system does not always give an accurate reflection of the health of the business. Using the cash-basis system can cause you to overlook signs of trouble.

If a number of clients have owed you money for more than ninety days, your business could be in serious trouble because accounts owed beyond ninety days are verging on the uncollectible. If you have a large bill coming due but haven't planned for it, you could be in trouble when your revenues don't provide enough money to cover the expense.

This is why it can make sense to project accounts payable and receivable out a few months at a time to make sure you're not going to run into trouble.

For many freelancers, this projection isn't difficult. They may have relatively few clients. They might receive two or three checks a month for their services. They can easily remember who owes what and when their clients usually pay. By the same token, freelancers tend to make relatively few purchases in a month and they certainly know when they're planning to upgrade their computer or if they've committed to a large purchase recently.

Nonetheless, officially tracking accounts payable items ("payables") and accounts receivable items ("receivables") can free up mental space for more important tasks. Keeping accounts payable and accounts receivable records helps you plan to pay business expenses and to collect from slow-paying customers.

Accounts Receivable Basics

Your accounts receivable journal (for amounts you're owed) should list the date you sent the invoice (if you allow thirty days for payment, the journal should reflect the due date), the name of the client, and the amount owed, plus an invoice number. I don't send many invoices so I just date them: Invoice 050519-01 is the first invoice sent on May 5, 2019; Invoice 050519-02 would be the second, should it be needed.

Update the journal each time you send a bill. When the money is received, simply mark the entry "paid." Be sure you also note the income on your general ledger when it is paid.

If you don't receive your payment when it is due (within thirty days), send a gentle reminder notice shortly thereafter, then another notice at fifteen days past the due date. At thirty days, a more strongly worded letter or a phone call is in order. Be prepared to consult an attorney should a receivable go beyond ninety days.

If clients are consistently late in paying, change your business practices to ensure prompt payment, such as requiring a deposit or billing partway through the project. Perhaps you could offer an incentive such as a discount for prompt payment.

For independent clients (not book publishers or book packagers, who expect to be invoiced after work is completed), I expect full payment before I begin working.

Accounting software, like Peachtree, and apps, like Wave, can help you with accounting and invoicing.

My invoices are very simple and I just write them as Word documents:

INVOICE #050519-01

Date: May 5, 2019
From: My contact information
To: Client's contact information

For: Developmental edit of Client's manuscript, TITLE, as agreed in the Project Quote dated March 15, 2019.

TOTAL DUE: $1,000,000.00
PAYABLE UPON RECEIPT

"Payable upon receipt" just means those are my terms — the client got the bill, now it's time to pay it. If you want to offer a discount for prompt payment, you can; if you want to threaten a late fee, have at it.

I have not actually collected one million dollars for a developmental edit but I do dream.

Accounts Payable Basics

Your accounts payable journal (for amounts you owe) should be updated each time you incur an expense. The payables journal should list the date the amount is due, who is owed, for what service or supply, the account category (use the account category you use in your general ledger, such as "AD" for "advertising") and the amount owed. Depending on how uneven your income is, you can project payables as far ahead as you wish.

Most business try to project payables about six months ahead, which helps them prepare for upcoming expenses. Trying to project more than six months ahead resembles guessing to a large degree.

As soon as you have paid a payable item, mark it "paid" in your accounts payable journal. Also note the expense on your general ledger when it is paid.

Note that an accounts payable journal is usually less important for most freelancers than an accounts receivable journal; you will always have outstanding invoices that you're waiting for payment on and the accounts receivable journal is an excellent way to keep track of them.

Retaining Documents and Records

In order to prepare important financial records, you'll need to keep certain documents, including receipts for expenses, bank statements, credit card statements, and invoices plus check stubs, direct deposit notices, and PayPal notifications from clients who have paid you. Designate a physical location for any piece of paper pertaining to financial aspects of your business and create a folder in your email program for paperwork that comes online.

Then, each day or once a week, depending on how much business you're doing, enter the information in your general ledger. Once you've entered the information, file the physical documents in a box or envelope marked "posted" and move the online notifications to a folder with the same designation.

If keeping track of two different locations for paperwork feels too disorganized for you, you can print out online records and file them physically, or you can scan physical paperwork and keep it organized in your computer. Most companies allow you to opt-in for email notification of bills and many businesses will email or text your receipt instead of printing it out.

Generally you will need to keep receipts (and other records relating to income taxes) for seven years. The returns themselves you will want to hang on to forever to prove you filed them.

Recording Financial Information

For the general ledger and accounts payable/receivable journals, you can use whatever works — a spiral notebook, a special computer program, or an app like FreshBooks. Your records can be lists you type in Word. It doesn't need to be complicated. As your business grows you may decide to use more sophisticated methods of recording your information.

Another possibility is to pay an accountant to set up an accounting system to suit your business needs (and to show you how to use it). This is usually the most expensive choice you can make (the professional fees can be written off) but is also the most personalized. If you're in doubt about how to get started, this can be a good choice.

Developing Recordkeeping Habits

Develop good recordkeeping habits right away. Keep all relevant receipts, canceled checks, bank statements, and credit card statements in one place. You don't have to update your financial records every single day of your life, as long as you do so regularly. If you at least remember to put business receipts in the cookie jar in the kitchen, when it's time to update the general ledger, you'll know where to find the information you need.

The IRS expects you to keep itemized receipts for all of your purchases. You can't simply guess that you spent eight hundred dollars in postage last year. You have to have the receipts to back it up. Receipts must include the date, the name of the business from which you purchased the service or supply, a description of what was purchased, and the total amount you paid in order for the IRS to accept the document as a legitimate proof of the expense. More on this in Chapter 7.

At first, you may find yourself tossing business receipts without realizing it. To counteract this problem, collect every single receipt you receive throughout the course of the day in one central location—your wallet or an envelope in your purse.

Then dump the contents into the cookie jar and sort it out later. By forcing yourself to collect every receipt, you'll soon remember to hang onto business receipts. Use whatever method you need to make certain you keep the records necessary for your business as completely and as accurately as possible.

Chapter 7

The Paperwork Part, Take Two: Taxes, Contracts, and Insurance

The IRS hates self-employed people, especially freelancers. They don't come equipped with crisp and shiny W-2 forms, they're always taking those pesky home office deductions, and their income isn't nice and predictable.

Sad to say, the IRS doesn't trust you. Therefore, you must make certain that everything you do in connection with the IRS is aboveboard and can be backed up with documents, signed testimony, and character witnesses. (Well, at least hang on to the documents.)

Earlier, I recommended keeping receipts, bank statements, and credit card statements. These are essential for proving that you did in fact incur the expenses that you claimed to have incurred and that you aren't understating your earnings.

Preparing the Return

Each year, at the end of December, make a copy of your general ledger for the year and keep it with all of the documents that support the ledger entries. Then when you're ready to prepare your taxes, you'll have all the information you need in one place. If your general ledger has been kept up to date, it may be all you need to prepare your tax return.

You can prepare your tax return in one of several different ways. You can bring the pertinent information to a tax accountant or tax preparer; you can use a computer program (I like TurboTax) to walk you through the steps; or you can sit down with a pile of forms and a bunch of informational booklets and do the deed yourself.

As with accounting, filing taxes is the kind of thing we're tempted to leave to someone else. But unless you understand, at least in general terms, how tax rules affect you and how your taxes are calculated, you'll be in the dark about important business considerations that affect the financial health of your business.

For example, many new freelancers don't realize that in addition to the employee's share of social security taxes, they are responsible for paying the employer's share (the so-called self-employment tax) and so they don't save enough of their income to pay the bill at tax time. Knowing your responsibilities is often the difference between successfully freelancing and . . . not.

If you use certain accounting software such as QuickBooks to keep track of your general ledger, the tax programs will simply import that information directly from your accounting system to your tax records, which makes the whole ordeal much easier.

Some business owners use tax programs like TurboTax, then ask their accountants to look over the results as a double check. (This is cheaper than getting the accountant to do the whole caboodle to begin with.)

If you own a partnership or corporation, it's wise to consult with an experienced tax preparation specialist in order to understand how to file your tax returns appropriately. Sole proprietors can also benefit from consulting with a tax preparer, at least for the first year. Discuss the information your accountant or tax preparer will need ahead of time so you can stick it all in a shoebox and present it to him or her at the appointed time.

Helpful IRS Documents

The IRS provides some handy information free of charge to business owners. These may be helpful in planning your tax strategies and preparation. Check out Publication 583, Starting a Business and Keeping Records; Publication 334, Tax Guide for Small Businesses; and Publication 535, Business Expenses. You can find these at **www.irs.gov**.

No Receipt, No Deduction?

What about those occasions when you don't have a receipt to prove you incurred a business expense? Maybe the receipt was accidentally thrown away or you didn't notice that the clerk failed to stuff it in the bag. Make a note of the expense, when and where it was incurred, and hang on to it. You can still deduct small expenses (technically, the IRS only requires receipts for purchases over $75 but it's much easier for you to keep track of expenses if you save all your receipts).

Independent Contractor Status

The government will agree that you're self-employed (an independent contractor) and entitled to business expense deductions only so long as you meet certain requirements. The IRS believes that many employees incorrectly call themselves independent contractors, which costs the government money.

Employees who claim business expenses when they shouldn't cheat the government out of tax revenue. Other problems also result. If everyone were an independent contractor, employers wouldn't have to pay benefits; provide leave; pay payroll and unemployment taxes; contribute to workers' compensation programs, social security, and retirement programs; supply office space, equipment, and coffee. It would be much cheaper for them. It would also leave many workers unprotected and exploited. (Not everyone wants to be a freelancer.)

Therefore, the IRS applies certain rules to make sure that an independent contractor (freelancer) is really an independent contractor. An employer can tell an employee when and where to work and how to do a job. An organization cannot do this with an independent contractor. The organization simply specifies the work to be done.

Of course, it's not as if this criteria makes it easy to distinguish between an employee and an independent contractor. The fact that you work at home doesn't make a difference (people telecommute and are still considered employees.) To avoid being reclassified by the IRS (and possibly having to pay more in taxes), you should:

- Work for more than one client (this is simply good business practice anyway).
- Maintain control of the project. The client shouldn't tell you who to hire (if you're subcontracting any part of the work) or how you do your job or when you should be in the office.
- Be responsible for maintaining your own office, paying your own taxes and insurance, and doing your own marketing.
- Have written agreements with your clients, specifying the job you will do, when you will do it, how much you will be paid, and other details as applicable to your business.
- If your business is incorporated or has a "dba" ("doing business as") name, you are more likely to be considered an independent contractor.

Most freelancers don't need to worry about being reclassified as an employee instead of an independent contractor (especially if they follow the above guidelines) but bear in mind that the more you treat the work you do as a business, the more likely your work will be viewed as a business by the IRS. (You're not allowed to deduct business expenses if the IRS thinks you have a hobby, not a business.)

Form 1099

When you work on a freelance basis, your clients don't deduct income taxes from their payments to you the way an employer does. That's your responsibility. If a client pays you more than $600 in a year (this amount changes from time to time), he or she is supposed to send a form 1099 to you and to the federal government early in the year for the previous year's work. These are supposed to be sent by January 31. (It's unlikely that an indie author will do this but corporate clients will.)

The 1099 lists the amount of money the client paid you. It is similar to the W-2 form that you receive when you earn wages. However, you cannot rely on receiving 1099s to know how much money you made in a given year.

When you receive a 1099, make certain it's correct. It should show your social security number (or Employer Identification Number, if applicable). It should also show your name and address, plus the total amount of money you were paid for the calendar year. All of this information should be checked for accuracy. If the 1099 is incorrect, ask the client to send a corrected 1099 to the government and to you.

The 1099B is used for bartered and brokered goods and services worth more than a specified amount. If you barter extensively in your business, you may need to use or receive these forms. Check the instructions, readily available from the IRS, or consult an experienced tax preparer.

Note that Paypal reports payments made to you to the IRS, so clients who use Paypal do not also need to send a 1099.

The Non-Profitable Business

Freelancers often assume that they must make a profit at their business in order to write off business expenses. This is not the case. The IRS doesn't care if you make money or lose money as long as you're running a business. It's just that if you lose money year after year, the IRS is inclined to think that you don't have a business so much as you have an expensive hobby. In general, the IRS may reclassify your business as a hobby if you don't turn a profit in three of five years.

If the IRS does come calling, in order to prevent your work from being reclassified as a hobby you will need to show a profit motive: that you devote a substantial amount of time to your business and that you run your business like a business. Save information related to marketing efforts, communications with potential clients, and the like.

Many experts suggest keeping a daily appointment calendar in which you note the number of hours you worked and what you did. The notes that you jot down on your calendar, to-do list, or daily planner regarding business-related phone conversations, errands, and appointments will also confirm that you're running a business, not a hobby.

Although you do not have to make a profit to write off business expenses (an exception is that you can't use the home office deduction unless you do turn a profit), it does help to make your case if you have some revenue or income from your business, whether or not your expenses are greater than this amount. Don't forget the small sums of money that people might pay you for various business-related reasons.

Also, don't forget that when bartering, the value of the service or product you receive should be considered income. Business expenses related to goods or services you provide in a barter are legitimate deductions. The IRS requires you to use 1099B to identify income that resulted from a bartered or brokered exchange. Consult this form and its instructions for information on determining market value for goods and services.

You've Made a Mistake

Suppose you file your tax return in April. Then you discover that you forgot to record three grand in income. You don't want to be audited. Now what?

The answer is simple: the 1040-X. Although the "X" seems sinister, it's not. It stands for the Amended US Income Tax Return form, which is a brief, two-page document that simply asks you to admit the error of your ways and submit the requisite check to make up for your erring.

Although I mentioned forgetting to record income, if for some reason you forgot to deduct that new computer you purchased, you can claim it as an expense on the same form and tell the government why you think you're entitled to the refund.

You may have to amend your state and local tax returns as well.

Audit Avoidance

Most people with regular jobs have about a one percent chance of being audited. You, on the other hand, are two or three times more likely to be audited.

This is because it's easier for self-employed people to hide money than it is for people with normal wage-earning jobs, so the IRS likes to check up on us. Self-employed business owners can hide money by accepting payments in cash and not reporting the income, by inflating expenses, and by reporting personal expenses as business expenses.

The IRS randomly audits business owners (they also randomly audit regular people, just not as often). Although the main reason for this is to see who's stealing (the government considers it stealing if you don't pay your fair share of taxes), two other important reasons include discovering where business owners are making mistakes, in order to educate them; and discovering where business owners find loopholes, in order to close them.

The IRS looks for certain red flags. When they see these flags, they're more likely to audit a business owner. ("More likely to" isn't the same thing as "will"):

- If you continually show a loss from your business, year after year, the IRS might get curious.
- If your business expenses are more than 60 percent of your income or revenues from business, that can be a red flag.
- The IRS matches up those 1099 forms with your tax statement to make certain you aren't misrepresenting the amount of income you make. If their addition and yours don't agree, that's a red flag.
- The IRS likes consistency, so if your income tax returns vary widely from one year to the next, they might investigate. This is especially true if you make tons of money one year and none the next and the explanation isn't immediately apparent (for example, you left your job to start a business). The IRS doesn't mind you increasing your income as long as you increase your tax payments too. They just hate it when you start making less money than you used to.
- Taking the home office deduction can sometimes trigger an audit, especially if it's in connection with another red flag, such as a sudden decrease in income.
- Incorrectly prepared forms can cause an audit. Even if you simply forgot to sign your return, you might find an IRS agent on your front porch.

Audits come in different forms. Sometimes the IRS will simply send a letter asking for clarification on a certain question. If your answer satisfies them, you're off the hook. If not, they may pursue the investigation, perhaps by asking you to send materials to back up your statements or prove your deductions. (Remember to always always make copies of everything you send so that you can send the documents again after the IRS loses them.)

Occasionally, you may be notified that you miscalculated your tax payment and you'll just be asked to make a payment to cover the difference (with interest and penalties if the IRS is feeling especially snippy). This is simply to say that not every audit is a full-scale field investigation where special agents come knocking on your door to take a look at your home office.

If you do find yourself on the wrong end of an audit, and it isn't something simple like you can't add and you owe $219 instead of $210, get an accountant or tax attorney who has experience with audits in from the start. Such professionals will often be able to resolve the situation without extensive trauma to you. Since they're neutral, they aren't likely to volunteer more information than is needed or answer questions about your lifestyle. (The IRS loves to ask questions about your lifestyle to see if you're living large and reporting small; they also love to sit there quietly waiting for you to break under the pressure of their cold gray stares and tell them where the unreported stash is located.)

As long as you keep accurate records and document the activities of your business with care, an audit is nothing to worry about. Although the IRS may disallow some deductions or otherwise find a way to make you pay for the audit, if you can show that you did not hide income or misrepresent expenses and that you acted in good faith, in a business-like manner, you may have to pay additional taxes, penalties, and interest, but you won't lose your business or go to jail.

The main problem auditing IRS agents discover when they tackle small business owners? Laziness. Yep. You know exactly what I mean, because you can't imagine anything more boring than keeping track of little pieces of paper and adding together rows of numbers. It's not as if recordkeeping is horrendously difficult to do. You just have to convince yourself that it's important (it is).

Estimated Tax Payments

The IRS doesn't like to wait for its money, although it will let you cool your heels waiting for your refund. When you were an employee, every paycheck was subject to withholding. Your employer estimated your tax liability based on your salary and a few other factors.

Then your employer deducted a certain amount of pay for local, state, and federal taxes as well as for social security and sent this money to the government. When you filed your tax return for that year, you simply adjusted the amount you had already paid to compensate for various factors. Sometimes you might have had to pay a little more, sometimes you might have gotten a bit of a refund. Either way, the IRS liked you because you were gainfully employed and your employer remitted a portion of your earnings on a regular basis.

Now that you're a freelancer, this is no longer the case. Your clients will not determine how much of your pay to withhold. They'll send you the whole check, and you'll squander it on mortgage payments and chocolate and then at the end of the year, you'll owe the IRS ten grand and . . . hold on. That's why the IRS wants — nay, expects — you to make estimated tax payments throughout the year.

See, they don't trust you not to squander all that cash. Besides, if you earn money in January and the government doesn't see its share until the next April, why, the entire country could end up in financial ruin. Do you want to be blamed for the collapse of the economy? I thought not.

The idea of figuring tax payments more than once a year is enough to make you get a job. (That's what the IRS wants you to do). But it doesn't have to be that hard. Remember, the IRS just wants its money on a regular basis. You can use a paper form and send your payment in or you can file your estimated tax statement (and make payments) online at the IRS website.

Quarterly Due Dates

Estimated taxes are due on April 15, June 15, September 15, and January 15. People call this "quarterly" but as you can see it is not. Note that the January 15 due date is the following year. For example, for income earned in 2019, you would pay estimated taxes in April, June, and September of 2019 and in January of 2020.

Basically you look at your general ledger, figure out your income (minus expenses) and determine the amount of estimated tax you owe. Form 1040-ES (which you submit with your payment) has a handy worksheet that can help you calculate your tax liability.

Of course, if you're making estimated federal tax payments, you may need to make estimated tax payments for state and local taxes as well. Check with your local and state government for their policies.

Other Ways to Pay Tax Liability

There are some ways around paying estimated taxes, such as not making a profit, although that may not strike you as a very positive plan. If you have a wage job, even a part-time job, ask your employer to increase your withholding by whatever dollar amount you determine is necessary to meet your tax liability. (The government doesn't care where your tax money comes from as long as it comes.) Then when you file your tax return, you will have already paid your share of the tax bill.

If you have an employed spouse, and you normally file jointly, you can have your spouse increase his or her withholding to cover the amount of tax liability your business will have in the upcoming year. This method works for sole proprietorships and general partnerships, where your business income is reported on your personal income tax statement.

Calculating Your First Estimated Payment

Hold on, you say. I have no idea how much money I'm going to earn in a given year, so how am I going to determine a withholding amount or know when to make estimated tax payments?

If you're just starting your business and have no idea what your income is going to be, then relax. Review your general ledger once a month. As soon as you have made five or six thousand dollars after deducting expenses, file an estimated tax statement and then keep them coming. (A good rule of thumb is to set aside 25 to 35 percent of your earnings for taxes).

Avoiding Underpayment Penalties

If you earned ten thousand dollars in your first year of business, the IRS assumes you'll make at least ten thousand dollars in your next year of business. So, to avoid underpayment penalties, they expect you to make estimated tax payments of 110 percent of the previous year's tax.

Note that if you have a special situation and make a lot of money one year but don't the next, you're not *required* to make tax payments of 110 percent. If your income dips, you pay the amount that matches your tax liability. The 110 percent is just to avoid underpayment penalties.

One note of caution: the main point is that the IRS doesn't expect you to make guesses (well, okay, it is called an *estimated* tax payment), but they do expect you to pay taxes in a timely manner. It's just that we get accustomed to filing tax returns once a year, so we think we pay taxes once a year, when this is not the case. If you're a wage employee, you pay taxes all year long; you just don't have to think about it.

The estimated tax payment paperwork required of small business owners is not that difficult or time-consuming. Discuss estimated tax payments with an accountant who can help you get started.

Contracts and Letters of Agreement

When you're starting a business, you may sign legal documents for incorporating, leasing an office, and the like. If you're unsure about what anything in a legal document means, review it with your lawyer before you sign it. If you do ask a lawyer's advice, make certain you consult one who has worked with small business owners and is familiar with contract law.

Your clients will expect some type of contract or agreement specifying the nature of the editorial work to be done and the fee. Consult with an attorney to discuss creating a standard agreement for the basic types of editing you do; the specific language you use is best left to a lawyer who has passed the bar in your area and can effectively guide you.

Some writers' and editors' organizations have templates that you may find useful as a starting point.

Corporations such as book publishers will likely have a standard contract they use for freelance work. Be sure you understand it before signing it.

Watch Out for These Common Problems

Sometimes publishers will send you a version of a contributor's/author's contract, which can have clauses that hold you responsible for plagiarism even though you didn't write the book. You have to be sure you understand exactly what you're signing! (Most of the time when I've encountered clauses like this, the company and I have been able to work out a mutually agreeable solution.)

Be aware that companies that aren't accustomed to working with intellectual property (that is, they don't normally hire editors) may offer vendor contracts that have lots of inappropriate clauses, such as a requirement for you to have workers' compensation coverage even though you're running a sole proprietorship.

Never let a client contact convince you that "that clause doesn't matter." It does. Negotiate the contract, even if that means you have to delay the start of a project. In other words, don't assume the contract they send is the one you have to sign.

Keeping Contracts Low-Key

For most of my editorial work with indie authors, I use the project quote as the "contract"; when the client accepts it (I ask for email confirmation), I consider the deal done. Since I require all payment in advance, I generally don't have to worry about trying to hold a client to some kind of payment deadline, etc.

If you do, you may want to work out a more formal process and get your lawyer's advice about the best language to use.

Letters of Agreement

If you don't want to rely entirely on a project quote to cover you, but you don't see the need to resort to scare-off-the-client legalese, you can use a less formal approach, which is to write a letter of agreement or a memo of understanding rather than writing a contract.

If you go this route, the clearer and simpler your language, the better. State the work you will perform, when the work will be performed, and how much the work will cost. You can also note cancellation fees and any specific points that apply to your business, such as the requirement of a nonrefundable deposit. If your client disagrees with anything in the memo, you can work out the misunderstanding before you get too far along.

A written memo of understanding (or any agreement) isn't going to make much difference if a client decides not to pay up. You're still going to have to decide if it's worth hiring an attorney/collections agency, but such agreements can be helpful at the start, to make certain both parties understand what has been arranged. That's why memos of understanding should be clear and concise.

However, the more complicated the arrangement, the longer the length of the project, and the more money at stake, the more likely it is that you should consider asking a lawyer to draft a contract. But for basic work, such as editing an author's novel, a memo of understanding should suffice. You don't need a lawyer to look it over if you feel it covers the key issues, but it doesn't hurt to get an opinion.

If you want to turn the memo into a contract by having the client sign it, feel free! Getting expectations down in writing so that all parties can see them is more important than the exact form an agreement takes.

What an Editorial Agreement Should Include

While I won't get into specific clauses you should include, I do recommend that any contract/letter of agreement cover these items (there may be others you'll want to include, based on your experiences and your lawyer's recommendations):

- The scope of the work (what you'll be doing and what the client can expect in terms of your availability for answering questions or doing additional rounds of editing).
- Deliverables (how you'll do the work, such as sending a revision letter or making a conference call).
- Deadlines (when you will do things and when the author will do things: "Author will deliver the complete manuscript by June 30, and Editor will complete her edit no later than July 21.").
- When and how payment is to be made and total cost (for indie clients, I expect payment

upfront; for corporations I may expect partial payment at contract signing and at various milestones throughout).

- For indie author clients, I also have a disclaimer stating that I have no copyright interest in the work and that the author is free to use any of my suggestions, edits, and ideas without reservation. This assures authors that their work is their work, and that I won't be demanding a share of royalties next year when the book hits the bestseller lists.

You may also want to include some language about what happens if the client is not satisfied with your edits.

Client Contract Requests

A client may ask you to agree to a confidentiality clause, which is perfectly legitimate. If working for them will expose you to their business secrets, they need to have recourse should you go blabbing everything you know to their competitors. The problem with some of these clauses is the broad and general terms in which they're written.

Specify that information that should remain confidential must be marked "confidential." The confidentiality agreement shouldn't include information you learned from a third party or from public knowledge. (You don't want to be held responsible for public knowledge, do you?)

The confidentiality clause should have a time limit. For example, there's no reason the details of an author's plot need to be kept confidential after the novel has been published.

One variation of this clause asks you not to reveal work you've done for a company. Ghostwriters routinely agree to this, editors more rarely. If you can't claim a client as a client, how are potential clients going to believe you know what you're doing? Think carefully before accepting such conditions.

Clients may also ask you to sign noncompete agreements. This is more common in coauthoring and ghostwriting than in editing. There isn't a single reason why you should sign such an agreement. If it's the only way to get the client to hire you, you'd be better off finding a new client. You have every right to earn a living from your work, and no one should try to control that, certainly not a client.

Contract Dos and Don'ts

If you ever have any questions about the terms of a contract, do not sign the contract. Simply say that you will need some time to review it and then get the advice that you need.

Don't let the client contact tell you what the contract "really" means ("Oh, the indemnification clause is just boilerplate" — no, it's not) and don't believe them when they say, "We never enforce the noncompete clause anyway." The contract says what it says and you're agreeing to abide by what it says.

That said, don't let fear of legal documents stop you. Educate yourself. Look up sample contracts and ask colleagues if they'll share samples of their agreements with you.

Just as it's unwise to leave your accounting to your accountant (remember all those bankrupt celebrities?), it's dangerous to leave your legal agreements to lawyers. Just because you hired a lawyer to draft a contract doesn't mean it says what you wanted it to say. You should know what you need to say and what problems you're trying to prevent.

Identifying Insurance Needs

As a freelancer, you'll have several insurance needs, both business-related and personal.

Some of the risks of running your business cannot be covered with insurance, or the insurance costs would be prohibitively expensive, or the risk factor is so small that it wouldn't be worth paying for coverage. Weigh the benefits and drawbacks careful before making any decisions.

Covering Business Needs

Sources estimate that more than half of small business owners, especially home-based business owners, have inadequate insurance or believe they're covered for certain problems although they're not. Be certain to check with your insurance agent (and read the policy, asking for help and explanation as needed) regarding the exact coverage you have.

Business Owner's Coverage

A business owner's policy is a package of different insurance types. Similar to homeowner's or renter's insurance, it covers theft and property damage to a business. It can also cover other basic business insurance needs, such as liability insurance.

If you work from home, you'll need a rider or special amendment to your homeowner's or renter's insurance. Incidental business riders, as these are called, can be tailored to fit your needs. A business owner's policy can also cover at-home businesses, although it's more expensive than an incidental business rider.

Some insurance companies offer special in-home business insurance plans that provide liability coverage (which protects you in the event of being sued), replacement of income (which provides income if something happens—like a fire—that makes it impossible for you to run your business) and regular property coverage for theft or property damage.

General Liability Coverage

Liability coverage is important if you rent or own business or commercial property. It's also necessary if clients or employees visit your home for business-related reasons. If you meet clients in your living room and one winter day a potential client slips on your sidewalk and breaks her ankle, she could sue you.

If you have a homeowner's/renter's policy, you may think that's enough (after all, the UPS driver could sue you, too, if he slipped on the ice while delivering Christmas presents, but no one seems to worry about that). However, some homeowner's policies won't pay if the liability is the result of using the home as a place of business.

Before making a decision, also consider your clients' requirements. Depending on how you run your business, your clients may ask you to have general liability insurance. This is common if you (or your employees, if any) will be working on the client's property or with the client's property. If you have employees, clients may also ask for proof of workers' compensation and unemployment insurance.

Property Coverage

Property coverage protects your business in the event of theft and natural disasters. For your business-related property, you may wish to consider replacement-value policies. Ordinarily your property is insured for what it's worth. An older computer might be worth two hundred bucks. That's what the policy would reimburse you should the computer get stolen.

But you're not going to be able to run out and buy a brand-new computer for that amount of money. And it's not like you can wait around to see what kind of a deal you can get on discontinued models in six months. You're going to have to replace that computer right away, and chances are it's going to cost you more than the computer you lost was worth. That's why you probably need replacement-value coverage, at least on some of the big-ticket items. This will cover the actual cost of replacing the property that was lost with similar property.

Property Risk Reduction

In addition to insuring your property, you can further protect it by reducing the risks associated with it. To reduce the risk of theft, install good strong locks and exterior security lighting. Invest in an alarm or security system especially if you have expensive equipment, live in an area with a high crime rate, or if other factors place you at greater risk for theft.

Natural disasters such as fire and flood can destroy your property. Be certain you guard yourself against these risks as much as possible. For fire risk, install smoke detectors. Keep important documents in a safety deposit box at the bank or at least in a fireproof box in the basement. Know where your fire extinguisher is.

For flood risk, keep that fireproof box in the attic, not the basement. As soon as the river starts rising, put a flood plan into action by locating and safely storing materials essential to the survival of your business.

Your insurance agent can give you specific pointers for protecting your business from loss and may arrange for a discount on your insurance premium for the risk-reduction steps you take.

Think through all of the property issues related to your business before deciding that you've done all you can in order to reduce risk. Losing a computer to a thief isn't just a matter of losing a valuable piece of equipment. It also means you lose records and data. What can you do to keep the loss of data from shutting down your business? Be certain you back up computer files to an offsite/cloud storage source at least daily so they can be reconstructed later.

What about taking your own property off-site? Some insurance policies cover as little as ten percent (or even none) of the value of property that you take away from your home or place of business. That laptop computer you bring everywhere might be insured when it's sitting in your living room, but not insured (or underinsured) when it's sitting on your lap at the coffee shop. You may need to purchase off-premise coverage. This can be a rider or an additional insurance policy.

Business Interruption Insurance

Business owner's insurance packages sometimes offer business interruption insurance. If a tornado levels your home office and not only do you have five years' worth of business records to reconstruct but you can't fill your clients' needs because you can't work in the bare lot that was once your house, you have a problem. Business interruption insurance kicks in with payments to help you make ends meet while getting your business up and running again.

Most editorial freelancers who use cloud storage for backup can get their business up and running right away, and probably don't need this coverage.

Professional Liability Coverage

General liability insurance protects you if your client breaks her ankle on your front step, but it won't help you in the case of professional liability. If you could be sued over your professional practice, you should look into professional liability coverage. For most editors, this is probably insurance overkill, but if you're involved in writing (such as ghosting and coauthoring), you may want to consider protecting yourself. Member organizations sometimes offer access to this coverage or can connect you with brokers who can help you find it.

Sure, you don't ever plan to defame people, but what happens if you don't think you have and they beg to differ? Although professional liability coverage can be important to have, don't advertise the fact that you have it. This is merely spreading the word that your pockets are deeper than they appear and could invite nuisance suits by individuals interested in seeing if they might get lucky this week.

Insurance for Employees

If you employ others, you should consider commercial policies that combine general liability insurance (for the client who breaks her ankle) with workers' compensation coverage (in case your assistant develops carpal tunnel syndrome trying to keep up with the amount of paperwork you generate) and unemployment insurance (for when you decide it would be easier to do it yourself and fire the assistant).

If you have employees, clients will expect you to have this type of insurance coverage. (So will your employees and the government). Be certain to get a certificate of insurance that you can copy and forward to clients.

You may also want to provide health insurance or other benefits to your employees. Insurance agents with experience in employee insurance plans can help you decide. If you do employ others, check local, state and federal laws for employment practices and guidelines you should know.

Business Automobile Insurance

Even though you have insurance on your vehicle (you do have insurance on your vehicle, don't you?) you may discover that you'll need an additional rider or a different policy if you use your personal vehicle for business reasons. Be certain you check with your agent and your insurance policy.

Umbrella Policies

Umbrella policies cover costs in excess of those covered by your underlying policies. Say, for instance, that your general liability insurance covers up to $200,000 in claims. But suppose someone is injured on your property and incurs $300,000 in medical expenses. The umbrella policy picks up the difference between your $200,000 liability insurance cap and the $300,000 in medical bills.

Umbrella policies are cheap because someone else is responsible for the initial liability (most likely, someone injured at your house will require less than $200,000 worth of medical care). Only under the most extreme conditions will these policies kick in. It's unlikely you would need such a policy as an editorial freelancer, but if you anticipate having clients visit your home for business-related reasons, you'll want to think about it.

Personal Insurance

For your personal peace of mind, you may need additional types of insurance that are often offered through employers, such as disability, life, and health. Since you don't have an employer anymore you'll have to supply these yourself, as individual policies (rather than the group policy an employer has).

Sometimes the fact that they will no longer have insurance coverage prevents people from striking out on their own. You don't need to go to that extreme. Coverage is available to individuals, although the cost may be higher than you paid while employed at a company. Here's what you need to know.

Disability Insurance

Disability insurance comes in two forms, short-term and long-term. It pays a certain percentage of your average income while you're unable to work (due to injury or illness). Usually, people who purchase disability insurance should purchase both short- and long-term policies. Short-term policies cover you soon after the onset of a disability, such as the first day of an accident and the second week of an illness. These policies may continue providing income replacement for six months or so.

Then, if your disability lasts more than six months, your long-term disability insurance will start. Long-term disability insurance may continue paying for years after the onset of the disability. You should coordinate the plans so that the long-term starts as soon as the short-term ends.

Short-term disability insurance is more expensive than long-term, because it is likelier that you will break your leg in three places and be off work for three weeks than it is you will succumb to a life-threatening disorder that puts you out of commission for a year and a half. These policies usually coordinate with social security and other benefits you may receive (such as workers' compensation).

If you have adequate savings to cover several months' worth of personal and business expenses, then you may not need short-term disability insurance. In this case, you would coordinate the long-term disability plan to coincide with the amount of savings you have.

Whether you need disability insurance depends on many factors, including your personal feeling of risk. As a freelancer, if something happens to you, very likely your business will fold. Without you, the business is nothing. This being the case, disability insurance starts to look pretty good.

You might consider your assets—savings, a car, a house that's almost paid off—and calculate how long you could keep afloat without income. If you have a gainfully employed spouse, this may reduce the risk you perceive. Of course, your gainfully employed spouse could be involved in the same auto accident that disables you, so that's no guarantee.

If you're in a partnership or corporation with other owners, you may decide that everyone should be covered by disability insurance so that the disability of one person doesn't destroy the entire business and with it the livelihood of the others. Check costs for disability insurance at different levels of coverage to help you decide what you should do.

The amount of coverage you purchase is usually a percentage of your monthly income. Because your monthly income may be erratic, this can be hard to calculate. You also need to cover any business expenses that might occur while you're disabled. If you purchased a new computer for your business using a business line of credit and then broke both arms in a freak rollerblading accident, your business would still have to pay for the computer although you would be unable to work.

Life Insurance

Life insurance pays your survivors after your death. It replaces your income, at least for a period, and provides cash to pay expenses such as your burial costs, debts, and taxes.

There are two main types, term and whole life insurance. Whole life insurance, sometimes called cash-value insurance, works something like a savings account. You pay more than the premium amount and the extra investment becomes available to you on retirement. These plans are rarely a good choice. If you need the invested money before retirement, you'll pay big penalties. The return on your investment may not be very good. You should purchase life insurance as life insurance. Invest for your retirement in a different way.

Term life insurance requires you to pay a set premium for a set period of time (a term). If you die during the covered period, the policy pays off a specified benefit amount. The premium should be guaranteed over the life of the term. It comes in various lengths, such as five years or ten years or even thirty years.

You can also purchase life insurance that is renewable annually. This starts out less expensive than longer-term plans, but as you renew the plan each year, it becomes more and more expensive. Such coverage works as a stop-gap measure but shouldn't be part of a long-range plan.

Check with different companies to determine their prices for different terms. You may qualify for special premiums if you're young, in good health, and have both parents living. If you're in a partnership or a corporation with other owners, you may wish to have all owners insured so that the death of one member does not destroy the business. If you have adequate savings and your survivors, if any, will be provided for out of your estate (you own your own home, you have investments), you may not need life insurance.

Health Insurance

The greatest concern of the self-employed is obtaining and paying for adequate health insurance. Because the US health insurance situation is in flux, it's hard to know what to expect. At the time of this writing, freelancers could access health insurance options (including vision and dental) on the healthcare marketplace (**www.healthcare.gov**).

There is no guarantee that this will continue, but even if it does not, you may be able to find group health insurance through membership organizations or through a spouse's employer.

If you're still employed, sign up for COBRA insurance as soon as you quit to go out on your own. COBRA is the acronym for the budget act of 1985 that requires businesses with more than 20 employees to give full-time employees the option of continuing their medical insurance for eighteen months after they leave the company.

You have to pay the full price for coverage (your employer may have contributed before but is not expected to after you leave the company). You will also pay an administrative fee of two percent of the cost of the premium.

After the eighteen-month period, you'll need an alternate health insurer. You should line this up before your eighteen months have come and gone and maybe even before you quit your job, depending on how difficult you believe it will be to find appropriate coverage at a reasonable cost.

You can also purchase an individual policy through an insurance agent. You will need to consider how large a deductible you are willing to settle for, how much total out-of-pocket expense you can reasonably handle, and what specific needs you have, such as dental or vision insurance or coverage for dependents.

Where to Get Insurance

All types of insurance — business and personal — are available through independent and affiliated agents, but make certain you have the right agent. The agent who handles your life insurance policy may not be the most experienced person to handle your business insurance needs. Your agent should be able to provide the coverage you need, not just try to talk you into the coverage he or she has available.

Your business insurance agent should be familiar with small business needs. If he or she often works with freelancers or at least home-based business owners, that's a definite plus. If you purchase several plans (such as business owners' insurance and life insurance) with one company, you will often be eligible for a discount on rates. Nevertheless, shop around and compare rates to get the best coverage possible at the most reasonable cost.

Conclusion

You Should Be Freelancing (Shouldn't You?)

You made it all the way to the end of this book, which means you have a pretty good chance of succeeding as a freelance editor. Persistence is probably more important than skill and craft combined when it comes to succeeding as a freelancer and you've just shown you have that!

Throughout this book, I've tried to be realistic about what being a freelance editor means. It's a demanding, skilled occupation. I didn't want to make it seem easier than it is. Although, let's face it, it's not rocket science. So I didn't want to make it seem harder than it is, either.

In the introduction, I talked about the freedom and flexibility that freelancing offers. And in the conclusion, I want to talk about its power.

When I look back over the past twenty-odd years of freelancing, I marvel at how long I've been at it — longer than I've ever done anything in my life. I love freelancing, of course. But I came to it out of need. I simply could not have held a staff job when my daughter was young. There is no job I have ever heard of that would have let me take the amount time I needed to be with my daughter while still earning enough money to pay the rent. I have no idea what I would have done. I suspect it would have included a cardboard box under a bridge.

For a long time, I thought I was something of an exception—the anomaly who tries not to be too obvious about how strange and different she is. And then I realized that many—maybe even most—of us freelance not because we're renegades throwing caution to the wind but in order to hold our lives together.

To be there for our children, many of whom have challenges.

To provide for our families when our spouses lose their jobs.

To make an unexpected early retirement into something more than squeaking by.

For us, freelancing is about much more than living life on our own terms. It is about making our very lives possible.

That's the power of freelancing.

Now and then I think about those people selling dreams of ocean-side cabanas and it makes me laugh. They have so completely missed the point.

But I hope you don't.

Want More?

Interested in learning more about the craft of editing?

Sign up for the Club Ed newsletter to get editing tips, learn new information, and find out when new classes, books, and white papers become available:
https://www.clubedfreelancers.com/the-resort-news/

Information about my classes and one-on-one coaching can be found here:
https://www.clubedfreelancers.com/adventures-excursions/

Join my (free) Facebook group for developmental editors, Club Ed:
https://www.facebook.com/groups/ClubEdGroup

Small Business Glossary

Account: The name for an entry in a bookkeeping or accounting record.

Accounts payable: Money owed by a person or business, but not yet paid.

Accounts receivable: Money earned by a person or business, but not yet received.

Accrual Basis: Method of accounting that records expenditures when they are committed to and records income when it is earned; the other main accounting method is cash basis.

Amortization: Spreading out the cost of equipment and supplies over a lengthy period, usually to meet tax deduction requirements.

Assets: Everything a person or business owns.

Balance sheet: Financial record that shows the assets of a business on one side and liabilities and capital on the other. The totals on each side of the balance sheet are the same (they "balance.")

Business license: Permit to operate a business, required of some businesses in some localities.

Capital: Equity or ownership interest in a business. The difference between assets and liabilities.

Cash flow: The amount of cash immediately available to meet business expenses.

Cash basis: Method of accounting that records expenditures when they are paid and records income when it is received. The other main accounting method is accrual basis.

Copyright: Ownership of a creative work, and the legal right to publish, sell and distribute such a work.

Corporation: Company with a business ownership arrangement that limits the personal liability of the owners.

Creditor: Person or business to whom payment for goods or services is owed.

Credits: Liabilities. See *Liabilities*.

DBA: "Doing Business As." Term applied to the fictitious name a business owner gives to his or her company.

Debits: Assets. See *Assets*.

Deduction: Expense that can be subtracted from earnings to reduce the amount of taxable income of a person or business.

Depreciation: The loss of value of goods that occurs over time, especially with goods such as cars and computers.

Expenses: Costs involved in running a business, including the purchase of goods and services, plus intangibles such as depreciation.

Fiscal year: A twelve-month period of business recordkeeping, usually the same as the calendar year.

General ledger: Accounting record that records income and expenses.

General liability: Potential legal obligation for damages to another person or another person's property.

General partnership: Type of business with two or more equal owners; the personal liability of the owners is not limited.

Gross earnings, *gross income*, or *gross profit*: Basically all the same thing. The amount received for a product or service in excess of the cost of producing it.

Income: Money received in exchange for labor or services.

Income statement: Financial document that shows income and expenses for a specific period of time.

Insurance: Indemnity or promise of protection against loss offered in exchange for a specified amount of money (a premium).

Invoice: A bill or statement showing how much is owed for a service or product.

Liabilities: Money owed by a person or business.

Liability: Potential legal obligation.

Net earnings, net income, or net profit: Basically all the same thing. The amount of money earned after all expenses have been deducted. The term "net net profit" is sometimes used to indicate the amount of money earned after income taxes have been deducted.

Net worth: Value of a business after its liabilities are subtracted from its assets.

Operating capital: Money used to finance day-to-day business expenses, especially necessary at the start when income does not meet expenses.

Outsourcing: Contracting with outside providers to deliver needed goods or services essential to the operation of a business.

Payables: See *Accounts payable.*

Professional liability: Potential legal obligation for damages incurred while performing one's profession.

Profit-and-loss statement: See *Income statement.*

Receivables: See *Accounts receivable.*

Replacement value: The cost required to purchase new equipment should a loss occur, rather than the actual depreciated worth of a piece of equipment.

Revenue: All money generated by a business, including income for services, earnings from interest, or money from one-time sales of assets.

Risk reduction: The act of protecting assets from potential loss.

Royalty: Payment made to the creator of an artistic work each time a copy of the work is used or sold.

Sole proprietorship: Simplest type of business ownership with a single owner in charge of all operations; the owner's personal liability is not limited.

Tax exemption: Special exclusion from paying certain types of taxes.

Write-off: See *Deduction*.

About the Author

Jennifer Lawler has worked for many years as a freelance book development editor on a wide range of editorial projects for traditional book publishers as well as independent authors—everything from cookbooks to memoir to paranormal romance to thrillers.

She launched Crimson Romance for Adams Media (which became an imprint of Simon & Schuster), overseeing all aspects of acquisitions, editorial, and production. She has also worked as a magazine editor for MSP Custom Publishing.

She is the author or coauthor of more than forty nonfiction books and novels, including her popular and award-winning Dojo Wisdom series (Penguin). She has written a number of romances as well.

She worked briefly as a literary agent and has taught in the biomedical writing program at the University of the Sciences in Philadelphia, the copyediting program at the University of California – San Diego, the Loft Literary program in Minneapolis, and far back in the mists of time, the English Department at the University of Kansas.

She earned her Ph.D in medieval English literature from the University of Kansas and a black belt in Taekwondo at approximately the same time. She hasn't quite decided which has been more helpful in her career.

Her website is at **www.jenniferlawler.com**.

Made in the USA
Las Vegas, NV
29 July 2021

27227734R00152